FEED YOUR HEAD

Some Excellent Stuff on Being Yourself

FEED YOUR HEAD

Some Excellent Stuff on Being Yourself

Written by
Earl Hipp

Illustrated by
L.K. Hanson

HAZELDEN®

First published June 1991.

ISBN: 0-89486-755-5
Library of Congress Catalog Card Number 91-70208
Printed in the United States of America.

Editor's note: Hazelden Educational Materials offers a variety of
information on chemical dependency and related areas. Our
publications do not necessarily represent Hazelden's programs.

About the author: Earl Hipp is a writer, speaker, and consultant.
He works with businesses, schools, parent groups, and other
organizations to help people manage life's challenges and get
along with each other better. He has written *Fighting Invisible
Tigers — A Stress Management Guide for Teens*, and three
pamphlets for Hazelden's *Step Meetings for Young People* series.
Earl is very interested in hearing from his readers. You may
contact him at the following address: Human Resource
Development, Inc., 333 North Washington Ave., #300,
Minneapolis MN 55401.

About the illustrator: L. K. Hanson, in addition to being an
illustrator and cartoonist for the Minneapolis Star Tribune, has
illustrated Hazelden's *If Drugs Are So Bad, Why Do So Many
People Use Them?* He lives in Minneapolis, MN.

About the kids who contributed: The personal stories in this
book are true, though some names have been changed to protect
people's identity.

A BIG ROUND OF APPLAUSE

A lot of people helped me put this book in your hands. Like me, they wanted to help make a positive difference in other people's lives, in YOUR life. So here's a big fat THANK YOU to:

- All of the young people who took the time to fill out questionnaires, make suggestions on the content, and openly share their experience, strength, and hope.
- Wendi, Antonia, and Emily for their honesty, and for keeping me from being too serious.
- More caring adults than I can list, like Misty Snow, Gary Legwold, Pat Mercy, Deb Meininger, Jane Donovan, Kate Nelson, Duane Hackbarth, Barb Olson, Mary Kassera, Deb Harley, Gail Gentling, Pat Ruddle-Dooley, Mark Kaufman, Lisa Jensen, Jane McDowel, Charley Murphy, and Ellen Albee — to mention a few!
- The Star Tribune newspaper for permission to use excerpts from their "Mindworks" series, an exciting forum where adults can read about young people's opinions on important topics.
- The staff at Hazelden, especially editors Sid Farrar, Joe Moriarity, and Vince Hyman, and designer Scott Zins.
- My supportive friends, who helped me get through the hard times and feel good about myself — all the time.

AND A GIANT THANKS to the artist, my friend L. K. Hanson, for his coolness under pressure, and for his ability to capture and illustrate the weird parts of life. For a smooth older guy, he has a wild kid inside him.

And finally, tons of gratitude to my Higher Power for the love I'm feeling in my life, for having patience with me, and for having a sense of humor.

EARL HIPP 1991

HOW TO GROW A PERSON

Everyone is in the business of becoming the best person they can. We are always finding out what we can and can't do, what's right and what's wrong, who we want to hang out with, how to handle our problems, how to deal with partners, who we can really trust, and how we are alike and different from everyone else. All this kind of stuff is just part of what we have to sort through every day.

With all this going on, you can feel really confused sometimes. And when you're feeling confused, as you already know, it can be very difficult to decide what's right for YOU.

That's why we put this book together, to help you make your way through the daily maze of questions, worries, ups and downs, problems and puzzles. We hope that you'll use it regularly for inspiration, hope, and support as you grow into someone YOU like and respect.

This book:

- **Won't** fix your big problems, change the world overnight, make you rich, cure diseases, or get your room cleaned. Reading about how to make a life isn't the same as going out and doing it.

- **Will** give you some new ideas, let you learn from other young people's experiences, help you ask the right questions, let you know you are not alone, encourage you to love and respect yourself, suggest some skills to develop, and most importantly, encourage you to reach out for help when you are up against more that you can handle.

HOW TO USE THIS BOOK

Open it at the beginning and read to the end.
OR
Open it anywhere and read the first thing that catches your eye.
OR
Look up topics that interest you and go to those sections.
OR
Check your feelings right now, and then go to THE FEELINGS INDEX in the back of the book. It will tell you where to look for help.
OR
Just pick out one of the titles that grabs you and go for it.

However you use this book, we think you'll find some excellent stuff inside that'll help you THINK, FEEL, and GROW yourself into a person you love and respect.

WHAT'S IN THE BOOK

(• = what kids say)
TOPIC INDEX WITH TITLES AND QUESTIONS

The Feelings Index

ELEVATOR MUSIC IN YOUR HEAD

Did you ever notice that in some stores, elevators, or malls, they play the same boring music at very low volume. It's a special type of music developed after years of careful research, and it's designed to put listeners in a relaxed and happy mood. This kind of music is *supposed* to be played softly so it will be just below your *conscious* level of hearing, just part of the background.

We all have a kind of personal "elevator music" playing in our head a lot of the time. It is usually made up of old "tapes" that contain "favorite" worries, self-doubts, and concerns. We've probably worked for years to make them.

(**SEE.** ☞ WORRY)

For example, when you read the word GRADES, a whole bunch of thoughts about grades will come into your head. It's like a tape with all your worries about your school performance just began to play. The same

SEX · SCHOOL · PARENTS · MONEY · FRIENDS · THE FUTURE · DRUGS · LIFE

is true with other words like MONEY, DRUGS, SEX, THE FUTURE, and on and on. If you just say one of those words and then close your eyes, you're likely to hear a whole "tape program" begin to play. The problem with listening too much to your worry tapes is that you start believing them. Soon, THEY'RE telling you who you are. Even if what you're worrying about never happens, you'll still spend a lot of unnecessary energy feeling anxious and afraid.

Because over time we have UNCONSCIOUSLY collected these worry tapes, they actually have a life of their own and can start playing at any time. The only way to deal with them is to create new, more positive tapes that cross out and replace the old, negative messages.

(SEE☞ GETTING A NEW COACH AND SELF-ESTEEM ASSESSMENT)

Once you've done that, you'll have to pay attention to that little voice in your head so you can CONSCIOUSLY "switch tapes" when you realize a negative one is playing. The goal is to have a positive program of messages *you've* chosen about yourself and your life playing as much of the time as possible.

> "What hurts me most is not the things others say to me. It's what I say to myself. I have this malicious little voice in my head that tells me, 'I can't.' It has the power to squash my self-confidence and rob me of all my talent, hopes, and dreams. It's the voice that keeps me from risking anything for fear of failure by saying (things like) 'Stupid me. Look, I blew it again. I can't do anything right.' "
>
> "Fortunately, I've found a way to fight it. When I find myself focusing on failure, filled with anxiety, I stop for a moment and remind myself of the truth. I do not become a failure because of one or any number of mistakes. I remind myself of all my successes and crush the voice that lies to me. Then I try again, this time with the support of the most important kind — from myself."
>
> —*Steve, 17*

2

What Kind of Self-Talk Do You Hear?

● "I'm pretty good at this."
— Ann, 17

● "I hear a lot of put-downs. Often the things I hear in my head are the same comments that other people jokingly say to me." — Devon, 17

● "How good I have to do in school." — Jeff, 17

● "I can do it, I can make it places, all I have to do is try." — Lynn, 16

● "I'm always telling myself to get my act together." — Jenny, 17

● "Negative most of the time, and when I do hear something good, the negative will follow it to change it, making my self-esteem lower." — Sara, 17

● "If someone compliments me, my inner-self tells me to act like I didn't hear it." — Ann, 14

● "I hear a lot of questions like 'Who am I?' and 'What do I want to be?' " — Kerry, 16

Getting a New Coach

Somebody once estimated that we talk to ourselves at a rate of about 300 words-per-minute. This can be a wonderful way to pass the time while you are waiting for a bus, walking the dog, or taking out the garbage, IF you have something helpful or entertaining to say to yourself.

If you want to do a little "self-talk" experiment, say one of these phrases out loud — I AM A LOVABLE PERSON, or I REALLY AM SMART — then close your eyes and listen to the little voice in your head — your "self-talk." If you heard great follow-up statements, you are a lucky person. That voice you hear is something like a coach, and there is nothing better than having a great coach who regularly gives you positive strokes.

(SEE ☞ ELEVATOR MUSIC IN YOUR HEAD)

Some people, however, have this totally negative coach that is always reminding them of what they are doing wrong, how they are messing up, and calling them "dumb," or "stupid." If you listen carefully to your friends, you'll sometimes hear their negative coach taking over. How to tell? When you hear them saying things like, "Oh, how could I be so stupid," or the ever-popular, "What an idiot, I should've known better."

Carrying on this kind of negative self-talk, whether in your head or out loud, is how you make yourself a loser. If you have a coach like this in your head, *fire the bum and get a good one!*

❝ *The goal is to have a positive program* **❞**
of messages you've chosen about
yourself and your life playing as much
of the time as possible.

What Self-Talk Do You Hear When You Say to Yourself: "People Like Me for Who I Am"?

● "Yeh, people really do like me for who I am, that is the only reason they could. I'm not a fake person at all. With me, what you see is what you get."
— Kerry, 16

● "Well, I hope they do 'cause I'm as good as I get." — Jeff, 17

● "Yeh, right! Outward appearances are everything. If you don't look good, people ignore you and treat you differently." — Catherine, 14

● "Not many people really know me." — Rolf, 14

● "People do like me for who I am. I am always myself. If they don't like me for who I am, they aren't worth it." — Lynn, 16

● "No way is that true because I have few friends." — Missy, 16

● "I'm fat and ugly and no one likes me." — John, 17

● "Yes, I am pretty in my own way, unique and smart."
— Sara, 17

● "Why would anyone like you for who you *really* are?"
— Michelle, 16

● "Bull!" — L. G., 17

● "I wish I was different, I wish I stood out in a crowd."
— Ann, 17

THE HUMAN VOLCANO

Have you ever been with a person who had just exploded with anger? It's an awesome and sometimes terrifying experience, especially when someone seems to go off like that with no clear reason or warning. And it can even happen with parents or teachers.

Anger is one of the most complicated of all our emotions to deal with. In some families, expressing anger is not encouraged and letting it out may even bring others' anger down on you. If this is how you have been brought up, you may have trouble even knowing when you're angry, let alone being able to express it. Anger, like any emotion, will cook along inside of you whether you express it or not. If you always stuff anger inside the moment it appears, you can be really angry and not even know it.

Some people stuff and stuff and stuff their anger until, like a volcano, they finally blow. But this

isn't anger anymore — it's rage. Rage is hard to handle because it seldom makes sense. It often ends up hurting everybody involved. Like lava from the volcano, rage can destroy whatever is in its path.

You can tell when you are dealing with rageful people when the INTENSITY of their anger is greater than anything you've done or said warrants. In fact, sometimes you don't have to do anything to get rage dumped on you. Rageful people just go off every so often, and whoever happens to be nearby gets covered.

Rage, like lava, also tends to go "downhill." It spills all over people who are more vulnerable and less likely or able to fight back. For example, parents can rage at their kids, older kids go after younger kids, people mistreat animals, and so on.

If you're really so full of anger that you've become rageful, you need help. You need to spend some time with a counselor or someone you trust who can help you look inside to discover and then work out your old angry stuff. Next you need to learn how to recognize your new anger as it occurs, and then work with it instead of stuffing it inside and ignoring it. Until you can do this, you may remain "dangerous" to be around.

When you hear the rumbling from a rageful person, it is probably best to leave them alone. Besides, you can't reason with a volcano anyway!

Sideways Anger

No one really wants to be rageful. So if you think your anger can only come out as rage, you may not ever feel free to let your anger out, even when you really need to. When you have difficulty expressing anger, you can get into some pretty weird behaviors to avoid dealing with it directly. That's when your anger gets out "sideways." That means pretending you're not angry, but not really being successful at it. Ask yourself if you have ever done the following when you were angry with someone:

- **Went away**. Gave him the silent treatment, didn't call or say much or anything at all when you saw him, or disappeared from his life for a while.

- **Got mean.** Got sarcastic and critical, made fun of her around others, reminded her of old screwups, stopped doing things for her.

- **Got even.** Purposely didn't show up for a date or meeting with him, got him in trouble with other friends, told secrets about him, became physically aggressive, or damaged something of his.

These are just some of the ways of expressing anger sideways instead of directly and up front.

What's more, there's a cost for these behaviors: relationships weaken; your attitude toward people, friendships, and even life in general goes bad; and you become less fun to be around. Worst of all, every time you do not directly express your anger, you move a little closer to becoming a volcano.

The Gift of Healthy Anger

Anger can actually be a gift you give to people with whom you're upset. It can be a way of letting them know that FIRST, you care enough about your relationship that you want to get things right. SECOND, it's a way to tell people exactly what you need from them to feel ok again. It's important to be as specific as you can about what problem or behavior is giving you difficulty. Maybe you'll want to try working together to figure out what can be done to improve your relationship. Whether or not things finally get worked out, you've at least let the person know what isn't working for you. You'll have probably gotten rid of most, if not all, your anger too.

Unless you learn to recognize and work with your anger, you'll continue to be sideways with it and things will never improve. Pressure will build inside you until, somewhere down the road, there will be an explosion of anger or rage.

 (**SEE** ☞ HAVING FEELINGS)

Given the huge costs of stuffing your feelings, taking the risk to share your anger *when you feel it* can be the healthiest thing you can do for both yourself and your relationships.

Is Anger Easy for You to Express?

How Do You Let People Know You Are Upset?

● "I have a temper, but you really have to annoy me to make me be angry. Otherwise I just pretend you're not there." — Loretta, 15

● "It's hard 'cause I'm a very relaxed person. When I bottle anger I get uptight, I would rather express it and relax." — Jesse, 17

● "I don't know, mostly I just get really quiet and answer every question 'no.' " — A. C., 17

● "If I can express it I usually do it in private or sometimes I ignore them. Then they know and ask me what's wrong. If I can't tell them, I write it on a piece of paper and give it to them."
— Jessica, 15

● "It is always easier to keep it to myself than tell someone. Now my brother, well that is another story . . . Whoa!" — C. C., 14

● "Yeah, because if I can show my friends I care, I owe it to myself and my friends to be honest with anger too." — Marcia, 17

● "It's hard to express, but if I don't express it, then it just gets worse and I will get madder."
— Steven, 17

● "Yes, because if I get mad it just comes out and sometimes I say things I don't mean because I'm so mad. People can tell I'm angry by my face, tone of voice, and how I do things." — Shelli, 14

● "I've gotten angry pretty easily since I can remember. My parents let me do it. But I have a problem expressing anger with acquaintances or sometimes strangers. Sometimes I'm pretty sideways about it, especially with people I'm not close to."
— Delia, 16

What Do You Do When You Are Really Angry?

● "Throw unbreakable things, beat the crap out of my pillow, yell, go be by myself and think it over, talk to a friend about it." — Jody, 14

● "I stalk around and stay really quiet. I call my friends and complain and just let my side of the story out." — Nick, 14

● "Sometimes I will go in my room and cry or I will just get smart with someone or maybe yell at them." — Loretta, 15

● "I play drums for hours without stopping." — A. C., 17

● "I go in my room and shut the door." — C. C., 14

● "I usually talk to a good friend about it and then I'll feel better." — Steven, 17

● "Start yelling. Sometimes I'll hit something or someone like my brother or sister." — Shelli, 14

THE PERFECT BODY

When the mind and body are at war, they no longer work together for the good of the whole being.
—Marcia Germaine Hutchinson, Ed.D.
Transforming Body Image

In the scenery of spring
there is nothing superior, nothing inferior;
flowering branches
are by nature
some short
some long

—*Zen proverb*

Stop for a moment and think about what your image of a "perfect" body looks like. Do you know where this image comes from? We live in a culture that places a high value on physical appearance and is obsessed with thinness. By looking at TV and magazines, you'd think the world is full of skinny, trim, and bouncy people. Yet this image doesn't fully

represent what MOST of us look like or act like at all. Nevertheless, the message we get is that if we aren't that way, we just don't measure up, that we are somehow inadequate.

It's a huge challenge to rise above these powerful influences, to learn to feel at home and happy with the body we were born with, *just as it is.*

Feeling good about our bodies is *not* about constant exercise, diets, and trying to reach *someone else's* idea of an ideal weight or shape. This path is a prescription for failure, and for feeling bad about yourself. A person with a healthy body image is able to look in the mirror and see a lovable, intelligent, valuable, and uniquely beautiful human being.

How are you feeling about your body right now?

Uniquely Beautiful

Feeling good about your body is part of being a totally self-loving person. Here are some suggestions for learning to love a great body . . . YOURS.

- Use affirmations. That is, regularly tell yourself positive statements like: "My worth and value as a person have nothing to do with my body size or shape," and "I am a uniquely beautiful person."
- Don't compare your body with anyone else's, and avoid people who give body shape and size too much importance.
- Don't subscribe to magazines that promote the "perfect" body.
- Make a change that suits YOU: try a new haircut, different makeup, a new style of clothes.
- Eat healthy foods and exercise both moderately *and* regularly.
- Wear clothes that are comfortable.
- Read a good book that can help you change your indoctrination on body image, such as: *Transforming Body Image, Learning to Love the Body You Have*, by Marcia Germaine Hutchinson, Ed.D., or *The Obsession: Reflections on The Tyranny of Slenderness*, by Kim Chernin.
- Find or start a body image support group.
- Every time you look in the mirror, say something positive like: "This is me and I like what I see."
- Surround yourself with people who love you *unconditionally* for who you are.

CHICKEN COURAGE

Courage is fear that doesn't control you.

—*Eleanor Roosevelt*

The only thing that is really constant in life is change. Change, however, is not something we always greet with open arms. On the contrary, we almost naturally try to avoid change because it means losing comfortable old ways. Change can bring confusion and create new, unfamiliar situations that we have to figure out how to handle. In short, change can often be very difficult and scary.

Remember how frightening it was to move up a new grade each year? New teachers, new things to learn, new kids in your classes, new homeroom, new almost everything. Bigger changes can bring even more anxiety. Beginning high school, moving to a new city, parents getting a divorce, or even something wonderful like having a new baby in the family can all be really

I don't think I'm quite ready yet.

▃▃▃▃▃▃▃▃▃▃▃▃▃▃▃▃

disruptive and threatening. Sometimes change is *so* scary that people will choose the PREDICTABILITY of a totally bad situation over the uncertainty of a new, unknown one.

The catch is that change, fear, and growth *all* go hand-in-hand. All changes involve breaking out of an "old" you and into a "new" one. Perhaps flowers feel some form of fear just before they pop up out of the ground into the sun. Chicks must be a little nervous just before they hatch. Babies at birth probably feel confused and scared during labor and delivery.

No matter where we are in our life, it seems as though there's always SOMETHING that's changing — and giving us a chance to grow. **Unfortunately, if we don't learn to accept and tolerate our fear of change and the discomfort of growth, we will remain "underground and unhatched" — unborn as a person.**

> *You gain strength, courage, and confidence by every experience in which you really stop to look fear in the face. You are able to say to yourself, "I lived through this horror. I can take the next thing that comes along." You must do the thing you think you cannot do.*
>
> —*Eleanor Roosevelt*

How People Grow

- **Change starts with endings** — That means letting go of some part of your life as it's been, letting go of the tremendous security you've had in the old ways. Change means looking fear in the face and doing whatever is necessary anyway. Fear of change is something to get through, not avoid. When you get better at change, you'll realize fear and excitement are close relatives. Sometimes you'll even be able to move from "uh oh" to "alrrrriight!" in a matter of seconds.

- **The confusion zone** — After you decide to move toward change and start taking those first few steps, you'll soon find yourself in the "confusion zone": no longer who you used to be, but not yet who you will be. This is when you are most vulnerable — you may feel like you don't know where you're going or quite what you're doing, and that you're at the mercy of unknown forces. Letting go of old ways means you're missing some of the familiar things that helped make you who you were: you're no longer from *this* neighborhood, no longer in *that* relationship, no longer have both parents at home, no longer have the same friends, no longer an only child. Things are just not the same anymore.

When you're in the confusion zone, it's a really good time to ask for help and support from the people you trust. Because they're not caught up in this change and turmoil like you are, they can still see you and your situation clearly — *and* they can remind you of what is still constant, positive, and right about you and your life.

- **New beginnings** — You can tell you're leaving the confusion zone when you still feel unsure and a little fearful, but are getting excited about the new stuff. You may not have your bearings yet, but you nevertheless believe you're capable, likable, and that life is worthwhile. You actually find yourself starting to enjoy the new things you're learning and experiencing. You are looking forward to the changes and your new future.

We don't always have a choice about change: sometimes it's forced on us by the decisions of others in our lives — parents, friends, employers, teachers, or whoever. But we *can* still *learn* from change if we're open, accepting, and self-loving. Even hard and painful experiences in our lives can be the source of tremendous growth — though it may not feel like it at the time! The most important tools for successful change are *liking yourself*, and a safety net of good *friends*.

(SEE ☞ WEAVING A SAFETY NET)

What Is the Biggest Life Change You Have Experienced So Far, and What Was the Effect on You?

● "My parents' divorced when I was nine years old. At first I was relieved, but after a little while I started to hurt. I was really afraid that my parents wouldn't even be friends, or that I would have to leave one of them for good. I joined a family change group at school to get some help." — Shelly, 14

● "I lost 60 pounds in my 13th year. I can't really explain the feeling, but when you lose that much weight it's like being in a whole new world." — Delia, 14

● "I was a huge alcoholic in the 7th-9th grades. In 9th grade, I went to treatment for it and I have been sober for three years now. It was difficult, but I just went right through it. Drugs had taught me to hide and be a phony; recovery has taught me how to be me and not be afraid of myself." — Marty, 17

● "Adapting to getting a father at age eight. I was very upset 'cause I felt mom was paying more attention to him than me. At first I wrote notes to my step-dad because it was weird talking to him in person. As time went on I got used to the change." — Loretta, 15

● "I went to high school. It's a big change, people are older here and it is different being the youngest one. I was scared at first, but I finally figured out that they're only people too." — Marie, 14

● "I went from believing I was the ugly duckling to liking the beautiful black woman that I am." — Jackie, 17

THE EYE OF THE STORM

Everyone, absolutely everyone, has times when their life is pretty rough. It's as though we're in a small boat tossing and crashing about on the ocean in the middle of a big storm. We feel vulnerable, without direction or much control over our fate, scared, and lonely. And as with a bad storm, when we're in the middle of a crisis we often feel like it will never end.

Fortunately, most storms — the ones at sea and the ones in our personal lives — don't last forever. They *do* tend to blow over, and learning to survive these storms is an important skill for getting a great life.

A hurricane is one of the most devastating storms, with winds often reaching well over a hundred miles-per-hour. Needless to say, they make a mess of whatever is in their path. But right in the middle of all the raging confusion is a wonderful, calm place where the wind is quiet and the sun is

shining. This place is called the EYE of the storm.

One way to get through the hard times — life's "hurricanes" — is to find life's "eye," a place where we can rest and collect ourselves before heading back into the struggle. There are a couple of ways to get into the EYE. One is staying physically healthy and calm. The other is *regularly* taking the time to boost your feelings of competency and self-esteem.

Recharging Your Batteries

When life is full of ups and downs and you are working hard to cope with challenges, your body gets strung out. You may feel like a cat who's been living in a neighborhood full of unfriendly dogs — on guard for danger all the time. Staying on guard takes a tremendous amount of effort, and eventually it will wear you down physically.

(SEE ☞ THE PHYSICAL SIDE OF STRESS)

It's important to sense early on when your body's "batteries" are getting low, and then to do something positive to recharge them. Here are three of many ways to help your body recharge physically:

- **Be physically active** — As strange as it seems, *reasonable* and regular physical activity really helps. It gets your heart pumping and sweeps out all those nervous chemicals your body makes when it's stressed.

- **Don't "drink" fear** — Too much caffeine creates some of the same reactions in your body as fear — tension, nervousness, and *stress*. It's easy to consume a lot of caffeine and not know it. Coffee is an obvious source, but caffeine is also a major ingredient in many soft drinks. If you're already in a crisis, drinking more stress is not what you need! If you are fragile and nervous anyway, the added stress of caffeine can push you over the edge.

- **Get quiet** — Healthy ways to temporarily find the eye of life's storms include taking a hot bath, listening to relaxing music, using a relaxation tape or technique, or taking a nap. Any other method that helps you become physically calm and to focus on something other than your worries is great too.

(SEE ☞ WORRY)

Build Up Your Self-Esteem

As the storms of life wash over you, you may become unsure of your strengths and your ability to successfully work through the situation you're in. The skill you need here is to sense when you are beginning to feel helpless, overwhelmed, or that you just can't handle things. At that point, call a "time-out" to build your confidence and self-esteem.

 (SEE☞ SELF-ESTEEM)

Here are a few ways to do it:

- **Focus on things you can be thankful for (your gratitude factors)** — It is important during the hard times to remember and stay in touch with what you like about yourself and with the parts of your life that are going well.

- **Share your fears with someone you trust** — A problem shared is a problem cut in half. Talking to another person will help you not feel alone with your feelings. Supportive friends can help you remember your strengths. And because they're not so closely involved in the storm, friends can also help you look at your situation more clearly and objectively.

 (SEE☞ SAFETY NET)

- **Remember that you have weathered other storms** — You are basically a survivor who has gotten through hard times before. And you have seen your friends get through them too. Remembering — *knowing* — that the storm will end can help you endure what is difficult now.

- **Focus on some of the things you are good at** — You may not be able to resolve your immediate challenges right now. Rather than letting yourself be swept up by feelings of incompetence, focus on and put a little extra energy in the things you *are* good at.

- **Ask for help** — Because our culture encourages us (especially guys) to be "tough" — to hide our pain and "go it alone" — we often forget about all the help that is right around us. Or even if we remember, we're afraid to ask for it. Having other people help out is a nice reminder that we *can*

ery often depend on others if we only let someone know we
eed them. Asking for help when it's needed is the normal
esponse of a psychologically healthy person.

Trying to have a life without problems is NOT the challenge.
That's impossible. Instead, it's discovering how to stay calm,
healthy, positive, self-loving, and in touch with others in
supportive ways while we work to solve the problems that come
our way.

*Although the world is full of suffering, it is also full of
the overcoming of it.*

—Helen Keller

66 *When you're feeling helpless or* **99**
*overwhelmed, share your fears
with someone you trust, and try
to remember you've weathered
other storms.*

THE ATTITUDE MAGNIFYING GLASS

I remember as a little kid I would enjoy playing with this big magnifying glass. Sometimes I did mean stuff like cooking ants by focusing the sun's rays. Other times, I would use it to make things like food, a cut on my arm, dirt, or words on a page look huge.

In somewhat the same way, what we focus our attention on also gets bigger or louder. Right now, for example, focus your attention on the bottom of your right foot. Suddenly you feel the pressure of the floor and your shoe where before you felt nothing. The same thing is true with your tongue in your mouth, background noise in a room, or the sensation of your butt on the chair. Whatever you put your attention on becomes a bigger or louder part of the present moment.

This principle also works with your attitude. If you focus your attention on how bad your life is going — all the things that are wrong, dumpy, unfair, sad, and hopeless — you'll eventually get fried like the ant. All that negative stuff will just get louder and louder. For some of us, focusing attention on the bad stuff becomes a habit and, after a while, negativity is all we can experience.

Focusing your attention on the good things in your life, however, turns up the volume on them too.

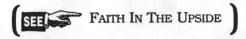

(**SEE** ☞ FAITH IN THE UPSIDE)

If you can make *that* a habit, your life will seem better, and the world will feel like a better place to live too.

Sometimes, the way we use our attention is the only thing we can control. Focusing on what's right will not fix the difficult parts of your life. But doing so will help give you a good attitude about yourself and your life. And that's the absolute *best* frame of mind to be in while working on your problems.

❝ *Sometimes I go about pitying* **❞**
myself, and all the time I am
being carried on great winds
across the sky.

—Ojibwa Saying

What Is Wonderful About Your Life?

- "Pretty decent family most of the time." — Missy, 16

- "Artistic talents, friends, family, hobbies." — Steve, 13

- "I have caring friends that are always there for me." — Ann, 18

- "My dog is choice and my job pays me money." — James, 17

- "My openness to others and my determination to stay sober." — Sara, 17

- "My attitude towards the future." — Lynn, 16

- "Being able to go to school." — Samantha, 18

- "My bowling and sense of humor." — Marie, 15

- "I have enough to eat and a family that loves me." — Jessica, 17

What Causes You to Feel Hopeless or Depressed?

- "Parents always nagging on me, my brothers always trying to start fights, and trying to be as good as my friends and then not succeeding." — Missy, 16

- "By being hurt or sad or telling myself that I screwed up and I am never going to get this or that right." — Lynn, 16

- "Anxiety, loneliness, and not enough attention." — Jessica, 17

- "Mostly myself I guess. I make me feel bad, or I let others get to me." — Ann, 16

- "That I'll never feel like a somebody." — John, 17

- "When a relationship breaks up with someone you cared about." — Nicole, 15

Being A "Serious" Junkie

I grew up with a lot of problems, so I became a person who was very, very serious. You could say I knew more about being a serious, worried, concerned, down, alone person than any other kind. Without realizing it, I had become skilled at being down. Getting down and serious was what I really knew how to do.

I guess it was because I was always so worried that I wound up with other serious people as my friends. We would hang out and get down together. We never had any real fun, mostly we just hung out and talked about what was wrong with people and the world.

You see, being up, playful, optimistic, silly, fun, and feeling great about myself and my life wasn't something I was very good at, and as a result, it was scary for me to be that way. I could only tolerate those "upside" feelings for very short periods of time before I would need to get serious again. It was comfortable to be serious; it's what I was familiar with.

It has taken me a long time to recognize and tolerate things that are right in my life — and to feel good most of the time. I began by consciously naming things I had that I could feel good about, and practicing letting in the positive feelings this created. I started with really little things, and over time I learned to feel up for longer and longer periods.

A strange change (strange to me, at least) also began — and it's still happening. As I am more able to experience positive feelings — to feel good about myself and my life — I find that different kinds of people are attracted to me. They're people more like the "new," positive me. A wonderful cycle has begun, because they in turn help me feel safer about letting go of seriousness even more and to just have more fun.

Sure, it's easy to be a "serious" junkie — we all have problems in our lives, and the world has certainly got some really big ones too. But if you are a "serious" junkie, you may have more choice about your attitude and experiencing the good stuff than you realize! Why not give it a try!

I can't speak for you, but for me, life is now better than it has ever been, and I believe it will keep improving!

(SEE ☞ CHANGE AND FAITH IN THE UPSIDE)

THE COURAGE TO DREAM

Living without dreams is like driving seventy miles an hour down the freeway right behind a giant semi, and not knowing where you are going. Because you don't know what's coming, you're never quite ready for changes in the traffic flow or route, or for danger. Things just seem to come out of nowhere and "happen" to you. You can only react, and usually you're a little late. It's really scary to drive like this, and scary to go through life this way too — not having any idea what's going to happen next or where you will wind up, not having any dreams or goals.

Yet it is easy to be caught without any dreams. If you have had dreams that failed to come true, disappointments in relationships, or parents that didn't follow through on promises, it can be easy to give up on dreaming — easy to not want to risk disappointment again, easy to give up hope, easy to give up on life.

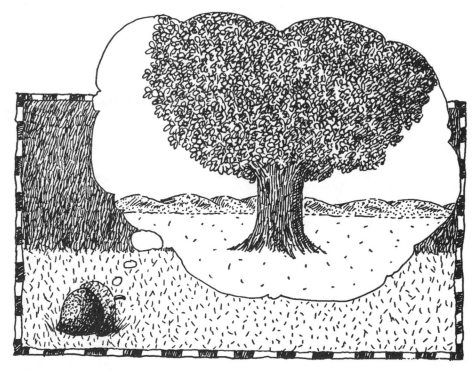

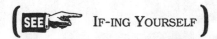

(SEE☞ IF-ING YOURSELF)

But it's our vision of what's possible — our dreams — that pulls us forward and gives direction and meaning to our lives. The courage to dream is one of the most important gifts we have. When you deny or give up on this gift, you can lose your sense of direction in life, and become too easily swayed by people who think *they* know the direction that's best for you.

Dare to dream. It doesn't matter how realistic you are at first; it's incredibly important to just do it. Isn't what we call a house today just an extension of what someone dreamed you could do with a tree! Isn't everything we use in daily life, from paper clips to a jumbo jet, just an extension of what someone dreamed might be possible, if you mixed inspiration with courage, some raw materials, and a little luck? In time, you'll learn how to dream more skillfully, in ways that lead to results in your daily life. As you find the courage to keep moving in the general direction of what *you* dream for *yourself,* you will be amazed at how the universe will move to support you.

❝ *Youth is wholly experimental.* ❞

—*Robert Louis Stevenson*

What Product or Tool Would You Like to Invent That Would Make Life Easier for Everybody?

● "A machine to stop time. I know this sounds stupid, but when I am fighting with my parents if we could take five — cool our tempers and then start time again to finish the discussion."
— Missy, 16

● "A time machine where you could buy time to rest."
— Kirstin, 15

● "A car what won't start if the driver smells like alcohol."
— Catherine, 14

● "A machine that I can walk into and disappear for a while or one that you can tell your problem to and it will tell you what to do." — Leigh, 13

● "Refrigerators and air conditioners that don't pollute the environment." — Steve, 13

● "A non-depression washer that you could walk through and come out happy."
— Samantha, 18

● "A product that makes new really clean water right out of what we just used in our homes." — Sara, 17

● "A combination personal garbage burner/energy generator." — Lynn, 18

● "A much more fair economic system that doesn't just benefit the smart and strong."
— James, 17

ll Steps

ou have a dream for yourself, no matter how wild it may seem, you can find a way to take a step toward its realization, even if the step is tiny. For example, if your dream is to live in the first human colony on Mars, a small, beginning step might be to go to the library for a book on the astronauts' experience of life in outer space. No matter what the dream, there is *some* step you can take toward making it happen.

As you continue to develop a dream for your life, you will get closer and closer to what is really important to you. In addition, you will learn lots about the world, and more importantly, what *you* want from life. Over time, this process of moving toward your vision becomes incredibly exciting because you can actually see your life taking shape.

Creating a meaningful life isn't easy, but neither are the options. If you think about it, you only have two other choices: to just let things happen to you, or to live out someone else's (parents', teachers', counselors', coaches') vision for your life. As long as you are living, breathing, and have a working brain, why not try to create something wonderful for yourself? It all begins with a small step toward your dream.

(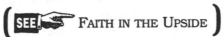 SEE FAITH IN THE UPSIDE)

" Who is driving your bus? "

—*Earnie Larsen*

What's Your Dream, and How Can You Move Toward It?

● "I would like to be a famous guitar player. I suppose I could practice more now." — Steve, 13

● "To be able to speak Spanish without effort. I can take more challenging language classes." — Lynn, 18

● "My dream ever since I can remember has been to be a veterinarian. I am good with animals and I love them. I could get a job at a vet clinic to see what it's like." — Kerry, 16

● "Live in California, be a super rich model with a great looking boyfriend. I can get a job and start saving money to get there." — Marie, 16

● "Write a book that gets on the New York Times best-seller list. Starting now, I can do more writing in my journal." — Devon, 17

● "I would own my own business someday and be in charge of everyone and everything. I can take business classes in college." — Mary, 18

● "To live in a great home with a great husband and two wonderful kids. I can try to get better grades so I can get a good job to help pay." — Missy, 16

● "My dream is to make it as an actress. I want to get degrees in psychology and acting. I can go to plays now to see what it is like." — Lynn, 16

● "Becoming an air traffic controller and living alone for a while. I can stick with my dream and work hard making it come true, because nothing comes without working to get it!" — Maggie, 15

31

WHY SOME PEOPLE USE DRUGS

You've probably seen a fly on a window pane trying to get outside. It will get up a head of steam, fly toward the light, and then smash into the glass. You'd think the collisions would hurt enough to make the fly stop. Instead, it seems to get mad and try over and over, harder and harder, to get out. It will bang its head until it's exhausted. It's like flies just don't see glass. If you see a fly caught in this dilemma, you can do it a big favor by opening the window and letting it out.

Sometimes we're like the fly when we keep hurting ourselves as we try to get to someplace that feels better. For example, if you're not feeling good about yourself or some part of your life, you might be tempted to use drugs to escape the bad feelings.

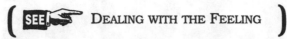

(**SEE** ☞ DEALING WITH THE FEELING)

Alcohol and other drugs may provide short-run relief from feeling bad. Eventually, however, using will cause you pain — and not just the physical pain of hangovers, sickness, withdrawal, or injuries from accidents or fights. You may also feel the pain of shame over what you've done while you were using and out of control, the loss of friendships, isolation, and the terror of a life that's spiraling downward. What's more, these feelings can hurt more than any physical pain.

Anybody can fall into this trap. If you don't have other ways to deal with your problems, you can find yourself using drugs again and again — in spite of the pain and bad consequences. Each time you use drugs, you'll think: *maybe this time it'll work, and I won't get in trouble.* But it *doesn't* work and you *do* get in trouble . . . and you keep using anyway. Like the fly banging against the window pane, you're just not able to see that what you're doing — repeatedly making the wrong choices about how to deal with your problems — is actually making the pain *worse*, not better.

After a while, you can lose your ability to choose any other way to deal with life. That is when you are addicted. You're not using drugs anymore; they're using YOU. By then, something much bigger than you has to come into your life to turn things around — to open the window.

66 *If you don't have other ways to* **99**
*deal with your problems, you
can find yourself using drugs
again and again.*

Have You Ever Known Someone Addicted to Drugs?

If So, How Was Your Relationship Affected?

● "My friend escaped to drugs. It did not work out as a friendship because she ended up lying and stealing all the time."
— Lynn, 16

● "My brother was that way. It made me feel distant from him. I was too young to help so after a while we grew apart and that is how we are today."
— Mary, 18

● "I had a friend who went back to drugs, so there can't be a relationship." — Christie, 16

● "I am a recovering alcoholic/drug addict. When I was doing drugs, I didn't have a relationship with anyone, especially myself. My drugs were my best friend and I did everything for them. You can't have a true relationship with anyone who is in a compulsive-addictive cycle." — Michelle, 16

● "I know someone who drinks when things start to get heavy. When that happens I have so much resentment because they won't face up to their problems and I get myself all upset."
— Debra, 16

A <u>Little</u> of John's Story

AT FIRST . . .

"I remember the first time I drank. I was fourteen and I was drinking beer I had taken from my father. Drinking my father's beer made me feel like I was older. The first time I got really drunk wasn't long after that. I remember the feeling of looseness and the giddiness it gave me, and I remember thinking, 'Wow, this is a wonderful feeling, I never knew that it felt like this.' It was kinda love at first rush."

LATER . . .

"There was a time when I came home totally loaded and climbed into the bunk over my little brother. He was harassing me and when I leaned over the edge to tell him to shut up, I just puked all over him. When my parents came home, they found my brother crying and me sitting in my own vomit trying to clean it up. My reaction was that I never wanted this to happen again. But to me that didn't mean quitting, just not getting caught. After that when I was really drunk, I just wouldn't come home."

EVENTUALLY . . .

"I'd get high by myself a lot of times. For the last month of my cocaine use, I didn't want anyone else to know how much I was using. I'd tell people I was going out of town for the weekend, go to my dealer's house, get the coke, and then lock myself in my room and just bump coke all weekend. When I would come down, it was like getting hit in the head with a two-by-four. It was real bad. Like plugging your body into an electric outlet and being zipped up for a long, long time. When you come down, it is like someone throwing you up against a wall, your body is completely drained, you can't sleep, your body is twitching, it is sheer hell. I couldn't talk, I couldn't function, I'd just sit and be quiet. I could barely get up even to pee."

FINALLY . . .

"After treatment I entered a halfway house. It was difficult at first because it was in my old neighborhood. But I just didn't call my old friends. I am going to my meetings (Twelve Step support groups), talking about my life, and working hard at building new support systems for myself. I have a lot more self-esteem, I know I'm a good person. I feel really lucky that my Higher Power is working to keep me sober and alive."

—John, 18

HAVING FEELINGS

Feelings are our emotional/physical response to what we think about and to what goes on in the world around us. *Everybody* has feelings — you can't stop them. But we're all different, and we respond to our feelings in different ways. See if any of these common responses sound like yours:

• **We may not realize we are having feelings.**

If, as we grew up, no one ever asked us how we felt about things, we probably didn't learn to recognize and talk about what was going on inside us. In some families, it's not ok to talk about how you feel about some — or even any — subjects. People who have this background are simply not able to identify and express what they're feeling. They often say they feel "funny," or bummed out.

• **We might go away from our feelings or pretend they don't exist.**

Events happen in our lives that stir up some

pretty intense feelings. If we are not able to tolerate and deal with the intensity and discomfort that come with our feelings, we may find ways to "shut down" emotionally. Some of us will find it safer to just put our attention elsewhere or somehow cover up our feelings. At other times, we may just try to look tough, to pretend nothing hurts or bothers us.

(SEE ☞ WAYS TO ESCAPE FEELINGS)

Feelings are what make us human, however. They happen whether or not we acknowledge them. Denying that we feel angry, sad, scared, or any other way just sets us up for bigger problems later. The emotional pressure will build and build. At some point, something has to give.

(SEE ☞ THE LOSS POT AND ANGER AND STRESS)

- **We can be aware of our feelings, name them, express them, and learn to talk about what we are experiencing.**

Feelings are a kind of information. They help us understand ourselves better. Feelings can also help us know how to live more successfully in the present. For example, if you feel fear, it might mean that something dangerous is about to happen — and that's a good thing to know! So in this case, you'd want to experience and understand your fear. In this same way, recognizing and experiencing other emotions can help you make better choices.

Opening up to your feelings will add a whole new dimension to your life. Often when we think of feelings, the difficult ones like fear and sadness come to mind. Certainly it's not fun to feel sad or scared, but as you grow in your ability to accept and work through the hard feelings, you will find your capacity to have pleasant, happy feelings will grow too. Your life will become richer and fuller. Developing your feelings vocabulary is a way to first recognize and then experience more of the wonderful person you are becoming.

(SEE ☞ ESKIMO FEELINGS)

"My stepsister had a lot of problems, and my mom was always having problems with my stepdad, so I got ignored. Mom was always trying to fix them. Compared to them, it didn't seem like I had any problems so I was left alone a lot. I would catch the bus by myself, do my own homework, and just take care of myself. I was supposedly a 'perfect child' in her eyes, but I was very lonely in my childhood.

"I became a kid who had to look good. I never knew how to share my feelings or even cry in front of anyone. I had to keep things together, I couldn't show there was anything wrong. I didn't want to be seen as being like my sister in my mom's eyes. I can remember when my grandma died when I was nine, it hardly fazed me. Sometimes I would cry to myself and just console myself, but for others I tried to look good."

— Dann, 18

"When I start to get down on myself for not doing enough or doing things well enough, I am tempted to either get real busy to go away from my feelings or to withdraw from people and go on a shame binge. Instead of feeding my face in those moments, I am learning to trust some people. I can call and tell them how I am feeling and what it's like. I ask them to remind me that who and what I am amounts to something, and that they care about me. Considering the hell I've lived through, I have to remember I am strong, and a miracle."

— Bonnie, 18

Ways To Escape Feelings

You can stay distracted from your feelings — from fear, hurt, anger, or any feeling that makes you uncomfortable — by overdoing just about any activity. If you are uncomfortable with your feelings, but things keep happening to stir them up, you'll find you have to do more and more to avoid facing your emotions. And you may not even realize how focused you are getting on your "escape" behavior.

The following list includes some of the ways people escape feelings by putting their attention elsewhere. These behaviors are — or can become — destructive and take over your life. If any of these situations sound like your life, don't be afraid to ask for help. Go to a parent, teacher, or school counselor and let them know what's happening to you. Keep looking until you get the type of help you need. In addition to these people, there are support groups made up of people who help each other recover from similar problems. You may find joining one that's right for you will be a big help too.

- Running or other physical activity for hours at a time, day after day.

- Eating, not eating, binging and purging, or just worrying about food all the time.

- Regularly taking hours to clean your room to keep it spotless, even when it's already clean.

- Thinking about other people's difficulties all the time: your friend's problems, your friend's friend's problems, and so on.

- Always wearing headphones and constantly listening to anything other than what is in your own head and heart.

- Sleeping all the time, especially when the rest of the world is awake.

- Too much television (some people think any is too much!).

- Taking baths or washing your hands every day, morning and afternoon or hourly.

- "Shopping till you drop" -- spending so much time at shopping malls they are like a second home.

- Becoming a video-games junkie, playing at every possible chance.

- Using drugs to get high, low, sideways, or generally detached from your body and life.

- Repeatedly leaving: leaving the room, leaving home, leaving school, leaving town to avoid the hard stuff. Wanting to be alone more and more of the time.

- A preoccupation with death, suicidal thoughts.

- Thinking constantly about anything, like nuclear war, your boyfriend or girlfriend, your grades, your health, your weight, your pimples, your future . . . you get the idea.

My Feelings

Being responsible for feelings means we take responsibility for what happens when we get out of control. If you are in a down and out, nasty, blue funk about your life, you have some responsibility for your impact on the people around you. If a friend says, "Boy, were you in a bad mood yesterday, I didn't like being yelled at," you need to own up. You might say something like, "You're right, I shouldn't have taken it out on you, and I'm sorry."

It is very hard for our relationships to work well when we don't know how one another feels. Sharing our feelings with someone tells them what is going on inside us. If we don't tell, we won't really know what is going on or where we stand with each other.

A safe rule for sharing a feeling with another person is to start out by saying, "I feel . . ." Using an "I" statement like this keeps you from blaming the other person for your feeling. For example, "I feel angry when you are late" is better than "You make me angry when you are late." The first statement says I am in charge of how I feel, and that your behavior (being late) is having a negative effect on our relationship. The second statement says the other person has power over my emotions and their being late messes me up — that I am a victim.

The great part about having feelings is that they are all yours. What's more, you can learn to be more in charge of how you feel if you want. It is ONE part of your life where you can make decisions about what you want for yourself. Then, if there are people who seem to be out to MAKE you feel bad, you can choose to ignore the invitation. It's great to be in charge of your own life in that way.

Eskimo Feelings

Because snow conditions are so important to Eskimos' daily lives and survival, they're very sensitive to different ways of experiencing snow. As a result, they have more than one hundred words to describe different kinds of snow. Most of us don't have to worry about snow very much. Even in snowy parts of our country, we have warm houses, and machines to push the snow out of the way. As a result, we don't have to pay as much attention to what kind of snow is falling. We can probably name only six different kinds of snow conditions.

Having ways to name your feelings is important too. If you don't pay close attention to your feelings and regularly express them in words, you lose the opportunity to understand yourself, as well as the chance for others to really know you. When people ask how you feel, you may only be able to say things like, "Oh, ok," or "Alright," or "Kind of down."

Learning to express your feelings is something like learning a new language. It may take learning lots of new words before you can accurately and fully describe your emotional experiences. The following are some "feelings" vocabulary words. How many can you use to describe what you are feeling right now? Remember, you can have many feelings going on at the same time.

afraid	alone	annoyed	amused
awful	awesome	bitter	together
belittled	bummed out	bored	confused
concerned	crabby	calm	cautious
content	disappointed	defeated	dumb
discouraged	eager	elated	enthusiastic
encouraged	enraged	excited	fearful
funny	furious	frustrated	great
gullible	glad	goofy	hopeful
hurt	attractive	hollow	hopeless
irritated	inadequate	interested	joyful
jealous	funky	lonesome	lovable
lost	mad	mushy	miserable
messed up	mindless	needed	nervous
overwhelmed	open	optimistic	paranoid

powerful	pent up	pushed	powerless
rageful	rejected	resentful	respected
sad	scared	safe	stupid
silly	shamed	shallow	surprised
tense	terrible	threatened	tolerant
unloved	unsure	unimportant	valued
victimized	wanted	worried	

Like building any new skill, it takes practice to get better at labeling your feelings. Sometimes you may even have to ask yourself, "What would it make sense for me to be feeling *right now*, in *this* situation?" to help you become more aware of your feelings at a given moment. With practice, patience, and support, you will come to better understand and express the wide range of feelings you can experience.

You may find that this process feels as though a part of you that's been frozen for a long time is finally thawing out.

 (SEE WEAVING A SAFETY NET)

❝ *Developing your feelings vocabulary* **❞**
is a way to experience more of the
wonderful person you are becoming

WHAT IS A FRIEND?

Friends don't grow on trees. Good friendships, however, do grow, and they take time to develop. You have to put forth some effort to make and keep friends. While there are no rules that friendships follow, there are some qualities that are really important.

The following are just *some* of the qualities found in strong friendships. The more of them you have in your friendships, the stronger they will be.

- **Equality** — In good friendships, both people contribute and consider one another equals.

- **Shared responsibility** — Friendships need to be cared for. In a strong friendship, both people feel responsible for it, and that means **both** invest their time and energy to make it work.

- **Trust** — Real friendship is based on mutual honesty and trust. One way to build trust is to take the risk of sharing more and more about yourself.

  (**SEE** 👉 PEOPLE I CAN TRUST)

- **Availability** — Good friends are around when you need them. Regular contact helps a friendship deepen. It's like caring for a plant: you can't just water it every now and then, and still expect it to grow.

- **Fun** — Friends should generally make your life more fun. It's true that you should be able to bring your hard and scary feelings into a good friendship and get support. But if you seldom bring your excitement, joy, silliness, humor, and playfulness to it, you have more of a one-person support group than a friendship.

- **Wide variety of interests** — High-quality friends are interesting — and interested in life. They're learning and growing and able to contribute to the relationship. Being bored together or always hanging out in the same place shows you have some things in common, but doesn't give your friendship much energy.

- **Alike and different** — Having some things in common is important. You automatically have ideas to talk about and activities to do together. But it is also important to have some differences. Friends who are different from you can bring out different parts of you, and help you discover new ideas and interests. Too much alike is boring; too different makes it hard to relate.

- **Loyalty** — Good friends will be with you when the going is tough. They can also give you room to be crazy and make mistakes. They will forgive your behavior and still like you. Real friends *don't* listen to gossip about you because they know and trust you.

- **Caring** — Real friends are interested in the details of your life. They remember stuff about you like your birthday and other special times. They remember your current fears and concerns, and ask you about them occasionally. They share in your joys, and hurt a little when you are in pain. They pay attention to your life, and let you know they care.

  (**SEE** 👉 WEAVING A SAFETY NET)

Each friend represents a world in us, a world possibly not born until they arrive, and it is only by this meeting that a new world is born.

—Anais Nin

One's friends are that part of the human race with which one can be human.

—George Santayana

A faithful friend is the medicine of life.

—Ecclesiastes 6:16

Two Things That Look Like Friendship But Really Aren't

- **Human Tumbleweed** — It is very possible to have lots of acquaintances, but no real friends. Kind of like a human tumbleweed, you cover a lot of territory because you don't have any roots. In fact, knowing thousands of people almost guarantees you *won't* have good friends because good friendships take time. "Human tumbleweeds" can be with people and still feel very alone because they are really just blowing across the "surface" of others. Making good friends means putting down some deep roots, really taking the time to get to know the other person.

(SEE 👉 WHAT IS A FRIEND?)

- **Just Being Similar** — Because you dress the same, talk the same, do the same drugs, play on the same team, hang out in the same places, or just do what other people do does not mean you are friends. Having things in common with another person is part of friendship, but it isn't what makes somebody a good friend. All "sameness" means is that you are like them — that's it!

> *"My friend Katie died in a car accident when she was eighteen. She always used to say to me that:* **'A friend reaches for your hand and touches your heart.'** *She was a good friend and touched my heart."*
>
> *— Ann, 18*

What Are the Qualities of a Good Friend?

"Caring, reliability, they don't talk about you behind your back, and they know your faults and still like you." — Jessica, 15

"Tells the truth, sense of humor, and no peer pressure to do anything." — Loretta, 15

"Honesty, humor, reliability, and understanding." — Shelly, 14

"Honest, trustworthy, likes to have a good time, acts as weird as I do, isn't snobby or conceited, doesn't whine, and doesn't feel stupid doing stuff." — Jody, 14

"It's just a feeling that is there." — Delia, 16

"They are real, patient, able to express their feelings, accepting, loving, understanding, assertive, non-manipulative, and honest." — Percy, 17

"Personality, originality, sensitivity, and a sense of humor." — Jesse, 17

What Is the Best Part About Having a Good Friend?

"That I can talk about most anything and that person will listen and understand and give me support." — Steve, 18

"A good friend accepts you for who you are and doesn't want or expect you to change or pretend to be someone you're not." — Shelly, 14

"Most of the time they are there when you are lonely or bored." — Loretta, 15

"You can share everything — hopes, dreams, fears, fun, and good times." — Jessica, 15

"Getting mad at each other and making up." — Percy, 17

What Is the Most Difficult Part About Having a Good Friend?

How Do You Get Really Good Friends in Your Life?

● "Being there for them and not getting too hooked into their stuff. Realizing that I can't change their life or them."
— Steve, 18

● "Trying to keep your friend forever." — Loretta, 15

● "Sometimes when you are too close it can cause friction or possessiveness with other friends." — Jessica, 15

● "When they move away, especially if you have known them as long as you can remember." — Shelli, 14

● "It takes time to build up the trust to have a really good friendship. Trust is the most important thing, and it doesn't come quickly." — Steve, 18

● "By being myself, being respectful, and putting out connecting energy." — Percy, 17

● "Starting with just a plain relationship and building it up over a period of time."
— Jody, 14

● "I have no idea." — Darrell, 17

● "Being honest and having good times together." — Loretta, 15

● "You have to be a good listener and be nice." — Marie, 14

How Do You Deal with Fights Between You and Your Best Friend?

● "It usually takes at least a few days to blow over. In the long run, it turns out for the best to talk calmly about why you got into the fight." — Jessica, 15

● "We try to talk it out and to understand the other person's point of view." — Shelly, 14

● "Argue, yell, get it all out, show every resentment and feeling, be real, don't play games. Then make up QUICK." — Percy, 17

● "If they're not willing to talk, I will wait a couple of days to let stuff cool off. Then I'll go back and try again, by then we're usually talking again."
— Shelli, 14

● "I get really mad and then try to see where they're coming from and try to talk to them rationally." — Marie, 14

● "We will usually have it out and then one of us will realize we're sorry and apologize."
— Steve, 18

● "We just yell or whatever comes out and then things usually are better than before." — Delia, 16

● "Just forget about the fight and pretend like it never happened."
— Jody, 14

THE LOSS POT

When we experience a major loss, the feelings that follow are called grief. Grief is actually many feelings that occur at the same time: sadness, confusion, anger, hopelessness, fear, loneliness, disappointment, helplessness, resentment, worry, and more.

Right after a major loss we experience a kind of shock. Many intense feelings pass so quickly — and sometimes change even from minute to minute — it seems like we're not feeling anything at all. As time passes though, things slow down a bit, and we begin experiencing our feelings more directly and deeply. Sometimes it takes months or even years before we're really back to feeling normal again, although we may never be completely the same person we were before the loss.

The degree of grief that you feel depends on the importance of the loss. You'll feel worse if your pet dies than if you lose your

house keys. The *same* feelings occur with each loss, but the intensity and duration of your grief will vary.

We can have major problems, though, if we don't have a way to express our feelings about a loss. Some of us can't cry easily, or aren't willing or able to talk about our sadness, anger, or fear. When we hold back feelings, they "cook" inside us. It's like all the grief goes into a big holding tank I call a "loss pot." Sadness from old losses gets mixed up with and added to new hurts, and it all just sits there in the pot making us generally depressed.

When we don't let our sad feelings out, our loss pot can get really full and spill over. That's when we

- can cry about anything.

- are depressed more often.

- are more fearful about things.

- have a harder time being playful.

- are not as hopeful about life.

- are not very open and receptive toward others

Carrying a lot of grief through life is like carrying a heavy load up a long hill. It takes a big chunk of our energy just to put one foot in front of the other. Just getting through a day can be difficult. We surely have less energy to put toward really doing our best.

If you can cry when you need to, you are really lucky. It's a great way to empty out your loss pot. Some people, especially boys and men, have been told that crying is a sign of weakness, but actually the opposite is true. Stuffing feelings into the loss pot is what makes you weak, as well as depressed, vulnerable, and closed-off as a person.

When you experience even a little sense of loss or grief, it's best to talk it out or cry with someone you trust. This person should be understanding and supportive. A close friend, parent, or counselor can be a good choice. In addition to keeping your loss pot empty, you will get to experience more of the complicated and wonderful person you are.

(SEE ☞ WEAVING A SAFETY NET AND HAVING FEELINGS)

Kinds of Losses

Because any loss can add to the stuff in the loss pot, it's important to be aware of situations that create even a little grief. Remember, even experiences that seem exciting or good can still bring the loss of "how it used to be." Happy and sad can exist together. See how many of these losses you have experienced. Then ask yourself, "Did I express my feelings or stuff them in my loss pot?"

- Death of a parent, relative, or friend
- Death of a pet
- Not getting invited to something
- Moving to a new place
- Loss of your physical ability to do things
- Parents divorcing
- Moving to a new school
- Losing a friendship
- Losing a favorite possession
- Breaking up with a boyfriend or girlfriend
- Being rejected by a parent or someone else important
- Getting a new baby in the family
- Loss of a freedom

Check out your feelings right now as you think about your losses. Think about what you can do now to express those leftover feelings and empty out your loss pot. Who can you share your feelings with?

66 *We are healed of a suffering only by* **99** *experiencing it to the full.*

—Marcel Proust

Have You Ever Had a Pet, Friend, or Relative Die?

If So, What Was It Like for You?

● "Yes, my friend Brett was killed, and another time my dog was put to sleep against my will. I felt like big parts of me were gone forever. I hated it and I felt very hurt, upset, mad, and angry for a long time."
— Sara, 17

● "Deep, deep sadness at losing a friend. The worst is when you'll be doing something and you'll remember them doing that same thing." — Tom, 15

● "When my friends died it was awful because they were so young and no one expected them to die. At first it was such a shock that I couldn't even cry, but when it sunk in, it felt so empty and lonely, I cried for weeks. I had a hard time believing they were gone forever. I still miss them all a lot, but it's easier." — Michelle, 16

● "Many people think that the death of a loved one makes you grown-up, but when my grandmother died, I didn't feel grown-up, I felt empty."
— Amy, 14

● "I have lost both a pet and a relative. I have a kind of numb feeling that never goes away."
— Ralph, 17

● "It was painful and I felt very alone and that nobody else knew the pain I was going through."
— Lynn, 16

● "I cried for a long time when my dog died. Then it was like I went numb. I called up some of my friends to help cheer me up and we went out and partied. I still miss him a lot even though it has been over a year."
— Catherine, 14

A Friend's Grief

"I am fourteen years old and two years ago my dad died. After he died, many people wanted to help me and my family. I found out that some friends knew how to help me more than others. Now I want to tell people what helped me and what didn't help, so they can be better friends to someone after a big loss."

Friends who didn't help

- ignored me.
- pretended my dad didn't die.
- asked me, "Why aren't you fun any more?"
- never asked me how I felt.
- teased me about not having a dad.
- never talked about my dad and never let me talk about him.

Friends who helped

- treated me the same way as before the death so I didn't "feel different."
- asked me how I felt and then listened.
- invited me to do things with their family.
- talked about my dad and let me talk about him.
- asked their parents to help with things that my dad used to do, like fix the chain on my bike.
- stood by me until I started to feel better, even though sometimes I was a real jerk!

66 *When you experience loss or* **99** *grief, talk it out or cry with a trustworthy, supportive, and understanding person.*

What Was the Biggest Personal Loss in Your Life So Far, and How Did You Handle It?

● "When my grandmother died three years ago. She was like my second mom because me and my mom lived with her for a while and we all grew very close. I was very hurt and I cried every time I saw something she had given me. Even though the whole family was together and upset, no one helped each other, we just toughed it through by ourselves. It's important to have a friend or relative to talk to in those times." — Loretta, 15

● "When I lost the false security of drugs. I was scared and was reaching out for a substitute. I found support in my AA group and other friends. They're better to lean on in tough times than a drug." — Patsy, 17

● "Breaking up with my girlfriend of two and a half years. I felt angry, sad, miserable, abandoned, and alone, like I had lost the most important thing in my life. I really started drinking a lot to cover up the feelings I had about it. I guess it's important to remember that things do get better eventually, no matter how bad they seem at the time." — Steve, 18

● "Yes, my friend died. I couldn't understand or accept it. I had seen her two hours before and suddenly she was gone. I felt like she was on vacation or just moved away. I thought that if I turned the corner she'd be there waiting for me. I felt guilty for any wrong I'd done her, but I loved her and she knew it."
— Ann, 18

Do You Cry Often or Easily?

● "If I can't handle what is going on, I go off by myself to cry. I feel better afterwards."
— John, 17

● "I cry when I get upset, which is easily. I guess I am just an emotional person." — Maggie, 15

● "I cry to let my feelings out, and I cry when I am happy or sad."
— Lynn, 15

● "Sometimes it feels good to cry. Sometimes all my feelings build up and a good cry lets them out. I don't cry at movies, I get choked up, but I only cry at my or someone else's situations."
— Ann, 18

WARNING SIGNALS

If you are a living, breathing person, you will sometimes have totally bad, rotten, stupid days — or even weeks. It's pretty hard to have all the pieces of your life working *all* the time. Like a bad storm, the hard stuff eventually blows over — but sometimes it's difficult to remember what the sunshine feels like when you are being drenched under a dark sky!

When we're really down, we can try and handle things ourselves (the hard way) — or talk to our friends (a great choice, if our friends are in a good place). Because we are least able to realize how bad off we are when we're at our worst, it is important to have friends who can recognize that we might have a problem. This means we also really need to look closely at a friend who's acting strange. Here are some warning signals people in trouble give. If any of your friends act in any of these ways **for more than a few days at a time**, they may be nearing

a crisis and need help:

- **Emotionally sensitive:** sudden anger or crying, seemingly little events or problems have a big impact, feelings easily hurt.
- **Always in the dumps:** overly focused on their problems, able to think only about what isn't working, a sense or belief that nothing is going their way.
- **Unexplained drop in performance:** grades falling, doesn't or can't do homework, late for work or doesn't show up at all, ignoring responsibilities at home.
- **Isolation:** avoiding people, secretive, missing school, avoiding parents, just wants to be alone all the time, not calling friends, not doing anything, nothing, no, negative, "just leave me alone!"
- **Change in sleep habits:** trouble sleeping, always tired, strung out, irritable, never rested, no energy or sleeping a lot, taking long naps, trouble getting up, sleeping in school.
- **Change in eating habits:** no appetite, eats and vomits, eats everything in sight, major weight gain, preoccupation with weight.
- **Major personality change:** suddenly behaving the opposite of how they've always been: a quiet person becomes wild and crazy, or a playful person gets quiet and withdrawn. Or other changes like these: bizarre ideas, seeing or hearing things that aren't there, losing old friends, picking new people to "be down" with, loss of the old self.
- **Heavy use:** of alcohol, other drugs, food, sex, rock and roll, and so on to escape reality.

(**SEE** ☞ WAYS TO ESCAPE FEELINGS)

Big Trouble

What would you do if you saw somebody waving a GIANT flag that said, "PLEASE, SOMEBODY HELP ME, I AM FEELING SO HOPELESS I JUST DON'T KNOW WHAT TO DO"? You would probably help, right? When someone's REALLY in the pits, things can be so bad that they can't even raise the flag. What they often do is send out other signals instead. Here are a few:

- Thinking (or just talking) a lot about death or suicide; even making actual threats.

- Behaving as though they're getting ready to die: giving away prized possessions, writing good-bye letters, or pointedly saying good-bye to people around them, writing a will, collecting pills or drugs.

- Talking like there is simply no hope for the future, like no one cares, like they've given up on life.

- Acting or talking like nothing matters any more — not parents, grades, friends, job, music, or activities.

If you see this behavior in a friend, just consider it a giant flag with **HELP!** on it. Even if they ask you to keep things secret, you **MUST** tell someone who can help. First let them know you care about them and that they are important to you, **AND THEN GET HELP**. It is foolish to believe that you can fix someone who's this far gone. It would be wonderful if you could save them, but you probably can't. And if you think you can, YOU may need help. **GET ADULT HELP, TELL SOMEONE RIGHT NOW!!!**

Are you getting the message?

We Keep Each Other Alive

"When a friend of mine committed suicide, I constantly harassed myself with questions about what I coulda done to keep it from happening. I know I am not responsible, and that my friend felt he had big problems. But no one knew 'cause we never really talked about stuff. I don't know why, but we just hung out together without sayin' much about how we felt about things.

"We knew we were good friends but we never talked about what we liked about each other or how we'd miss each other if anything happened. I kinda wish we'd have done more of that now 'cause it might have made a difference. I did say some things to some of my other friends at the funeral, told them they were important to me. I guess you never know when what you say to someone just might make the BIG difference. Sometimes I guess, we keep each other alive."

—Bart, 16

Responsible *To*, Not *For*

We all, at some time or another, slip into a dark and gloomy view of things. During those times, we need to trust that our friends will be available.

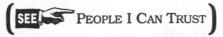
(SEE ☞ PEOPLE I CAN TRUST)

Being a good friend to someone in need means we are responsible **TO** be there to give support. That is a lot different from being responsible **FOR** solving that person's problems. When a friend is suffering and asking for help, all you can do is show you care and lend some support. In the end, your friend will have to find his or her own solution.

Here are some ways to support a friend who is having major problems:

- **Take the person and the problem seriously**. It may not seem like a big deal to you, but for your friend it may be huge. If you take your friend seriously, she may be willing to share more.

- **Be a good listener.** It's amazing how just being able to share your problems and fears with another person makes them easier to cope with.

(SEE ☞ HOW TO GROW HUGE EARS)

- **Don't give advice.** You may know what *you* would do in a similar situation, but you aren't your friend, and you simply can't really know what he's up against.

- **Share your experience.** This is different from giving advice. When you let a friend know you've had a similar problem, she won't feel so alone. Common experience builds trust, and seeing that you have survived can help your friend feel more optimistic.

- **Encourage your friend to talk to others.** Steer him to others who have had a similar problem, or to a support group. Sometimes it makes sense to get an adult point of view, or even professional help.

- **Let your friend know you care.** Your friend may not want to talk to anybody, including you. But even then, it can mean a lot just knowing somebody cares. Hang in there for her — send a card or call once in a while. It's all part of what

it means to be a real friend.

If your friend feels so bad off that he or she threatens or even talks about suicide, **take that friend seriously! DO NOT KEEP TALK OF SUICIDE A SECRET — GET HELP IMMEDIATELY,** and let your friend know you need him or her to be alive. Sometimes, one person can be the difference.

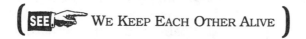

(**SEE** 👉 WE KEEP EACH OTHER ALIVE)

Over-Helping Friends

It is hard to see a friend hurting with big problems. We would do anything to help our best friends. We want to just make their problems go away. But it can be dangerous — for both you *and* the person you want to help — if you get too involved.

You might want them to be ok so badly that you make it a personal mission to get their problem fixed. Maybe you start worrying about them all the time, or living as though you had their struggle. Worst of all, if you feel responsible for them getting better, you'll feel bad and your self-esteem will suffer if they don't.

Our interference in a friend's problems can also be a subtle way of saying our friend doesn't have the ability to fix him or herself. Telling others how to live might also be a way to feed *our* ego by having others feel incompetent. Saying things like, "why don't you just . . ." can make your friend feel extra bad when they can't or don't want to live up to your expectations.

Some of us use worrying about others' problems as a way to hide from our own pain, or from the parts of our lives that aren't right. We may then find that the more difficult our life gets, the more we have to find others to fix. By living this way, we will feel doubly strung out. The more we worry about others — and the more we ignore *our own* problems — the worse our own life will get.

Our challenge as a good friend is to be with our friends as they work *their* way through *their* problems. In some cases, the pain they experience is the exact ingredient necessary for their growth. Just being there, caring about them, being willing to listen and to remind them of their value every once in a while, *is* doing a lot. It really is! And it also happens to be all we really *can* do for each other.

Have You Ever Had Friends with Huge Problems?

If So, How Were You Able to Support Them?

● "I have a friend who is getting into drugs. I talked to her about it but I don't think it was much help. Mostly, she knows that I'll always be there for her to talk to if she wants." — Lisa, 16

● "I have had different friends who were dealing with pregnancy, rape, abuse, death, abortion, drug and alcohol problems, living on their own, and so on. I could go on forever. Mostly what I can do is give them a shoulder to cry on and share my experience if it's related. If they need more help, I refer them to support groups, clinics, or other people I trust."
— Michelle, 16

● "All kids have problems. When I have problems, I want them to hold my hand, put their arm around me, and give me a big hug. I want them to just listen to my problems, I don't expect a solution, just support."
— Ann, 18

● "I have a friend with big problems getting along with her parents. She has trouble with teachers too. I gave her time and was understanding to her and didn't criticize her for how she felt. I tried to be there if she needed anyone. I support her and don't worry about myself when I'm with her. I would want the same back if I had her problems." — Mary, 18

● "I had a friend who was really depressed 'cause of problems with the principal at school. She came to talk to me and my mom about it. I tried my best to help her, but apparently it wasn't enough 'cause she tried to commit suicide. Thank God it didn't work. I tried my best, but she needed more help."
— Missy, 16

TWO MOUTHS— ONE EAR

Being able to really hear what others are saying doesn't just happen because we have ears. With so many things going on in the world around us, and all the chatter inside our own heads, it's amazing that we are able to stay focused on what other people are saying at all.

We usually know, however, when people aren't *really* listening to us. They keep looking away, seem hurried or distracted, ask us to repeat stuff, or keep the conversation focused on themselves. It's like they don't really care. These people seem as though they have two mouths and one ear instead of the normal design. It is almost impossible to build a strong friendship with someone like this — someone who can't or won't listen.

But being a good listener is exactly what we need to do if we want to be a good friend. By listening carefully to others we show our interest in them. We're telling them that we want to be involved with them. It's like a compliment. Listening carefully means we care enough about our relationships that we really want to understand our friends, to know who they are, what they think, and how they feel. Good friends have really "huge ears."

How Can You Tell If Someone Is Not Listening to You?

How Does It Feel When Someone Doesn't Listen to You?

- "They bring up their own topics in the middle of your thought, or never ask questions about what you are saying." — Lynn, 18

- "They have that blank look on their face and their eyes look very distant." — Karen, 15

- "They look everywhere but at me, and when I stop talking, they start a totally different topic." — Sara, 17

- "They answer vaguely. Like I can tell my parents are listening when I say something and they just go, 'O.k., but . . .' and change the subject, which is something they do all the time." — Michelle, 16

- "They have no idea five minutes later what you had just told them; they pick at their nails and shift positions a lot." — Ann, 18

- "It feels like they think they are better than you so they don't have to really listen." — Nicole, 15

- "It makes me really mad, especially if I am talking about something that is important or that hurts." — Lisa, 16

- "Frustrating — What's the point of sharing something with someone who's not interested?" — Lynn, 18

- "I feel dumb and ignored big time, like I don't really matter." — Sara, 17

- "I feel like grabbing them and shaking them into reality." — John, 17

- "It hurts." — Devon, 17

How To Grow Huge Ears

You can improve your hearing by cupping your hands behind your ears (literally making "bigger" ears). In the same sense, you can improve your ability to take in what others are saying — by increasing your listening skills. But like any skill, becoming a great listener takes study and practice. Here are three listening skills you can try with your friends.

Reflective Listening

This kind of listening is appropriate when friends are worried, frustrated, confused, or talking about something else important. It's a way to help them get a better understanding of their problems — and feel supported by you at the same time.

In reflective listening, you just repeat back to your friend what she seems to be saying. You function like a mirror: she expresses her thoughts, and then hears them echoed back and affirmed by you.

An example might be:

YOUR FRIEND: "I am so nervous and confused about the math test, I can't even start to study."

YOU: "It sounds like you're so nervous you don't know where to begin!"

While it may not seem like a very dramatic way to help, this process — your friend expresses her feelings and you reflect them back with understanding — helps her feel she's not alone with her concerns. Also, hearing our thoughts reflected back to us gives us a chance to look at them from another perspective. We can then decide if we are saying what we really think or feel.

Emotional Listening

This listening skill provides a way to communicate your understanding and acceptance of someone's FEELINGS. In emotional listening, you communicate that you hear and understand how he or she *feels*.

Examples of your responses might include

"I hear that you are angry about what happened . . ."

"I can understand why you might feel . . ."

"It sounds as though you're worried about . . ."

67

"It sounds like you are afraid for your friend . . ."

"You seem to be pretty sad about . . ."

"It's really cool that you are happy about . . ."

Feel-Felt

After you've made it clear that you understand what your friend is feeling, you can add another phrase to ease his sense of being alone with his feelings. You can do this by including him in a larger group, saying things like

"I have felt the same way too."

"I can understand how you feel; *no one likes that.*"

"I've known lots of people who feel that way."

These skills, along with eye contact, asking questions, and open body language, all let your friends know you're present and there for them — and that you really do have "big ears."

66 *Being able to really hear what* 99
others are saying doesn't just
happen because we have ears.
Like any skill, becoming a great
listener takes study and practice.

Do You Have Any Special Listening Techniques?

● "Watch them as they talk, keep occasional eye contact (if you constantly look at them they will become uncomfortable). Ask questions about the people and events in the story they're telling." — Lynn, 18

● "I try to put my own problems aside for a while and empathize with what they are feeling. I share similar experiences of my own which lets them know that I understand what they were experiencing. Besides making them feel good, it helps me to take my mind off things for a while." — Nicole, 15

● "I don't have any special techniques except knowing that they need me to listen and it's part of being a friend." — Kerry, 16

What Can You Say to Someone Who Isn't Listening?

● "Say something wildly irrelevant about elephants and cowboys or something, until they wake up." — Maggie, 15

● "Saying, 'Excuse me, but if you aren't going to listen I don't want to waste my air.' " — Kirstin, 15

● "Nothing, I'd stop talking with them." — Steve, 13

● "How would you feel if you were saying something important and I didn't listen?" — Ann, 14

● "Excuse me, but I'm talking to you," or "Would you please listen to me?" — Leigh, 14

STUCK IN THE MUCK

Shame is feeling that we are basically worthless — that no matter what anyone says, we are inferior and less qualified to breathe than anyone else on the planet. Shame can be the result of events that have happened to us, things we have been taught about ourselves, or something we've done. Shame refers to our lack of value as a person, and s*hame is always a lie!* It's a lie because *everyone* has value, worth, and gifts to bring others and the world.

(**SEE**  TOTALLY LOVABLE)

Feelings of shame are very hard to undo, often taking professional help along with a lot of support from our best friends.

Guilt is different: it's about things we've done that go against our values. When we've lied, cheated, stolen, or hurt people, for example, we are *supposed* to feel guilty. Guilt reminds us we need to own up to our choices and

actions, apologize, make amends, or find a way to forgive ourselves. Taking action to undo the guilt we feel about something we did gives us a way to feel good about ourselves again — even if what we did took place a very long time ago. Undoing guilty feelings as soon as we can lets us spend more time liking ourselves. It's a process that builds self-esteem and hopefulness in our lives.

When we uncover the lies hiding behind shameful feelings, or accept responsibility for actions that produced guilt, we're taking very good care of ourselves. It means we're making a choice to not be "stuck in the muck," a choice to not spend our lives feeling bad about ourselves.

WHAT KIDS SAY

Do You Ever Have Trouble Feeling That You Are a Wonderful and Lovable Person?

- "Yes, whenever I hurt somebody, I feel like I'm not such a great person. I feel guilty because I know that's not the way I am."
— Mary, 18

- "Yes, I feel that way when I look back and examine all of my downfalls and notice my bad qualities. I need to balance my good and bad qualities and realize that a little of each is normal."
— Lynn, 18

- "There was a time when I thought that everyone was better than me, and I didn't really know who I was. So I wanted to be like everyone I looked up to. I wasn't my own person, but I was a little bit of a lot of others."
— Kerry, 16

- "In my mind, I've always known I am lovable but I always worry about what others think."
— Rebecca, 16

- "I think everyone has trouble feeling good about themselves at one time or another. I know I get down on myself really hard a lot. But when I do I have close friends who simply tell me to get off my 'pity pot' and that they like me." — Michelle, 16

How Does It Feel to Keep a Secret About Yourself?

● "If it's about my stuff, it feels heavy. I ache so bad sometimes to tell someone, but just when I think I'll burst if I don't, something happens and I chicken out. I get so afraid of what people will think of me if they know what I've done."
— Michelle, 16

● "It mostly feels so bad! Like when I skip school and my parents ask me about it and I lie to them. It's like you have this huge, heavy weight you have to carry around and it's almost a relief to get caught." — Lisa, 16

● "It depends on what the secret is. If it's supposed to be a surprise for someone, then you feel good. If it's my stuff, it's sometimes painful to keep it."
— Devon, 17

● "Depends on whose secret. If it's my own, I feel locked up and put away. If it's someone else's, I feel good because it makes me feel trustworthy." — Jenny, 17

● "I would steal money from my six-year-old brother which was mean 'cause he doesn't come across money that often. My conscience bothers me, but I never say anything because I don't want to hurt him."
— Nicole, 15

Have You Ever Told Someone You Were Sorry for Something, or Has Anyone Ever Apologized to You?

How Did It Make You Feel?

● "You feel much better after everything is straightened out. You feel like a load is taken off of your shoulders."
— Maggie, 15

● "It depends on the situation, but usually I'd think that it took a lot of guts for them to come back and say they were sorry."
— Kerry, 16

● "I remember telling my best friend that I was sorry after we were in a fight that had lasted three months. Now we are inseparable. When somebody apologizes to me I think that that person is the greatest and has all the courage in the world and the biggest, loving heart. It lets me know they really care."
— Debra, 16

● "I feel closer to a person that says they're sorry, like they had let their guard down for me."
— Sara, 17

● "I'd respect them more because it was very big of them to fess up to whatever they did because apologizing can be very difficult." — Kirstin, 15

GETTING WINGS

Parents sometimes forget what it was like to be young, and young people sometimes forget parents are human and therefore not perfect. All parents screw up sometimes, and some even make a mess of parenting, really hurting their kids. But most parents do the best they can with what they've got.

Some of the most difficult times come when you want to test yourself in the world, use your own judgement, and do things your way. Even in the most ideal situations, it's still a tough call for any parent to know whether to let go or say no. That's why the tensions between parents and their adolescent kids are often so hot. It's because parents care, and because they're scared.

You want to try things to test your wings, and yet you're scared sometimes too. When do you need a parent to set limits, to take care of you when you're down, or cheer you on? When do you need them to let go, give you a push, and even allow you to make your own mistakes? Amazingly enough, for thousands of years (or maybe forever!) no one has ever known, FOR SURE, what's the best thing to do.

PARENTS

Even after we've left home, most of us want our parents' love, care, and support — AND AT THE SAME TIME, we want their permission and support to be a separate person. This conflict gets easier as we get older, but for a lot of us, it never goes away completely.

When you're making a "fly — don't fly" choice, you'll probably feel pulled in two different directions. One is toward your trust in your parents' experience and your knowledge that they really care for you. The other is toward your trust in what you feel in your gut, in your own intuition. Try to find a balance between the two. If you think you are ready, you can say so. Remember, these are not easy moments, and some conflict is NORMAL.

Here's a positive goal to strive for in times like this: really listen to each other, respect one another, and then do what you gotta do. The ground has a way of teaching us too, when we're learning to fly!

 (SEE☞ THE GIFT OF HEALTHY ANGER)

When I was a boy of fourteen, my father was so ignorant I could hardly stand to have the old man around. But when I got to be twenty-one, I was astonished at how much he had learned in seven years.

—Mark Twain
Essays: Advice to Youth

Most parents think they know better than you do, and you can generally make more by humoring that superstition than you can by acting on your own better judgement.

—Mark Twain
Essays: Advice to Youth

What Do You Fight About with Your Parents, and How Do You Deal with It?

● "Rules, my limitations, their expectations, my reactions, mostly we disagree about ME! I throw temper tantrums, pound up the steps, slam the door, and build a little more on the wall around my heart and mind."
— Jody, 14

● "A major disagreement is about how 'in charge' of my life I should be. I think I should have more say so, and my parents disagree. We try to reach some compromise, but it's not easy."
— Shelly, 14

● "My father is alcoholic but will not admit it and that affects everything. Sometimes talking helps, but then you just have to make your own way. I usually argue with him, but that just goes in circles. I just don't do what they want if it seems crazy or really unfair."
— Delia, 16

● "Grades, my friends, chores, using the phone, lots of little disagreements about basically everything. I sometimes yell. I know that doesn't help but I need to let my anger out some way. I also call my friends a lot. They have similar 'Parents Are Unfair' stories and it helps to talk it out with someone."
— Jessica, 15

● "Mostly about me being more out on my own. They realize like I realize that I am a very sweet person and they don't want me to go through the hardships they went through. When my mom worries, I tell her I love her dearly and that I'm a grown woman and that I can handle it, and if not, I know I can come to her." — Jackie, 17

About Parents

"I had just started becoming rebellious toward my parents when my father died. I realized shortly after his death that what my siblings and friends had told me about parents was wrong. Parents don't hate us. They don't bring us into this world to make our lives miserable. They bring us into this world to make us happy, to care for us, to love us.

"Respect your parents and their decisions so when you're older you won't regret how you treated them when you were younger. Parents do know what's best, most of the time."

—Kevin, 17

"Always ask. You may not get the answer you want or expect, and you might not even get an answer at all, but you should always give it a shot rather than guessing and assuming.

"I recently started to ask questions because we're moving and I have a right to know what's going on since the outcome will affect the rest of my life. I have a lot of big, hard decisions to make and I need all the facts so I don't make a bad one. But still I hold back because I know answers can be very painful and hard to accept. But I also know that once everything is said and done, I'll be glad I asked. Don't be left in the clouds. Always ask."

—Anna, 14

"I would like to hear 'I love you' from my parents, because I never hear it enough from them. Either they're going somewhere or they're gone when I get home. They seem to say 'I love you' to my nephews and nieces but when they get to me it's 'Joe, sit down.' And my parents should tell me more."

—Joe, 13

"The hardest thing is losing that certain closeness that you used to have with your parents when you were a little kid. They think that you don't want them to hug you, kiss you, or even tuck you into bed at night. The 'I love you's' seem to become less frequent because parents feel that adolescents think that it isn't hip for parents to show affection towards their maturing kids."

— Leigh, 16

PEER PRESSURE

Why Is It Called Peer *Pressure?*

To apply pressure is to apply a force.

One industrial use of pressure is to force soft and pliable materials into molds to make objects that all look the same.

Peer pressure is a type of force applied to get us to do something everyone else is doing.

The more insecure, confused, and alone we feel, the more pliable we are, and the more willing we are to be like somebody else. We all feel like this some of the time.

Pressure to conform can be pressure **not** to be you, but to instead be like everyone else.

If we all conformed totally to peer pressure, we would all look the

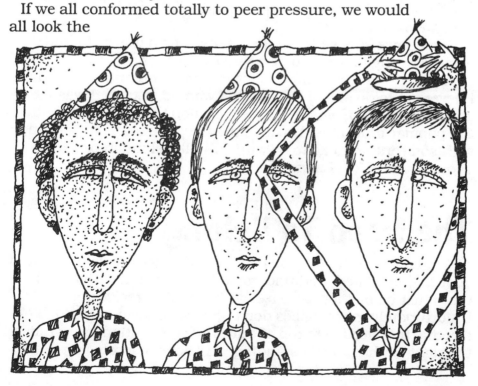

79

same, talk the same, think the same, feel the same, and do the same things.

Pretty boring!

What's Hard About Peer Pressure?

Peer pressure . . ."is scary because sometimes it seems like what you think is right is pulling at one of your arms and what other people think and expect of you is pulling at your other arm. Sometimes it's just hard to make the right decision." — Carol, 13

"The pressure that comes from peers makes more than just a temporary dent in people's lives. It can make a permanent, lifelong impression." — Sarah, 15

"For me, just saying no didn't work in the end. When the odds were 24 to 1, it became pretty scary. I forgot about my parents' warnings. I forgot about the commercials on TV, and forgot about my own beliefs. All I could think about was the drug. I knew it could hurt me, but that didn't matter any more. What mattered was being one of them." — Jennifer, 15

"Asking advice from friends is fine as long as you do what you want to do, not what your friends want you to do. I love my friends and value their opinions, but it's not their life I'm living, it's mine." — Doris, 17

"Sometimes kids sacrifice their sense of what is right and what is wrong in order to be popular." — Michael, 10

"Another bad thing about following the popular crowd is that I never got to do any of the things I wanted to do — I was afraid to tell them what I wanted. So don't hang around with the popular crowd just because they're popular. Hang around with someone you like to be with. You'll feel much better about yourself." — Rachel, 14

The Need To Belong

We all need to feel that we belong — that we are valued, cared about, appreciated, and understood. This is a healthy need that must be met for us to feel good about ourselves. Unfortunately, our families don't always do such a good job of meeting this need. On top of that, the competition over grades, the right clothes, social standing, and school sports can make us feel like an outsider even among our peers.

(**SEE!** ☞ TOTALLY LOVABLE)

If you feel left out of the "right" cliques, you may be tempted to find any clique, just to belong. You may find yourself doing stuff, saying stuff, even *being* someone you aren't. But there is another choice here. You *don't* have to get caught between belonging to the "wrong" crowd and not belonging anywhere.

You'll feel like you belong if you spend time with people you truly enjoy for being themselves, people whose values and behavior feel good to you, people who are doing things you enjoy and feel are right for you. That means *building friendships* with people who will like you *regardless* of what you wear, where you come from, what you look like, or any other outside, surface stuff. It means seeking out people who are comfortable enough with themselves to accept you for being creative and different and YOU. It may take work to find friends like this, but it's worth it.

(**SEE!** ☞ WHAT IS A FRIEND?)

And if you're true to yourself — if you're "real" — you may find that the people you're looking for will somehow just show up in your life! Because they're attracted to you!

Certainly, you'll always need courage to discover and be yourself — ask any young person or adult who's tried it. But being totally yourself — being real — is truly the best way to go through life. People who support you as you try to be honestly you each moment will be your best friends in the long run. And *you'll* be a better friend by giving that support to them in turn.

To be nobody but yourself, in a world which is doing its best, night and day, to make you everybody else, means to fight the hardest battle which any human being can fight, and never stop fighting.

—*e.e. cummings*

Why Do People Get into Cliques?

● "To have a group of people to count on. They are a close knit group of friends to talk to and to do stuff with. It's dangerous if you can't be yourself, though. If you are just being yourself and people accept you for that, then they are your true friends. See, anyone can be accepted by groups for pretending to be someone they're not — but only people who are themselves find true friends." — Nick, 14

● "Often it is for a sense of belonging. I think it is stupid, though, a set-up for peer pressure. What's the difference if you're a beautiful person in Nikes or in sandals, you're still a beautiful person." — Jesse, 17

● "Because they are not sure of themselves. I don't think it's right but I do it. The benefit is being accepted and the risk is being pressured into something you don't think is right." — C. C., 14

● "Because they don't know which end is up and they don't have a clue about life. I laugh, because they actually believe THEY know what life is all about. I don't either, but I don't pretend to." — Delia, 16

● "I don't think you go to school and say, 'Ok, I want to be with these people or those people.' You just start talking to people and all of a sudden you're friends. The benefits are lasting relationships, the risks are choosing the wrong crowd to hang out with." — Loretta, 15

FAITH IN THE UPSIDE

Do you ever feel that a lot of bad stuff just happens to you? That somehow the universe is dumping on you? That life is nothing but hassles with parents or brothers and sisters, problems with school, no money, best friends turning against you, no transportation, and that even the dog seems to be ignoring you?

If you spend too much time nursing the attitude that the universe is out to get you, that attitude can become a permanent belief — something like a religion. Here's how it can happen. In the beginning, you generally expect that bad things will happen. More and more you only notice the bad stuff. Pretty soon you really believe the bad stuff's coming, and eventually you'll actually have a *faith* in the downside. Your fears and worries become like prayers for bad things to happen

— and lo and behold, they do.

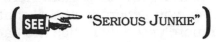

(SEE☞ Getting a New Coach)

Would you believe it's just as easy to have faith and expect that the universe is out to do you good? Even during the worst of times, there are many good things in your life along with those troubles. But recognizing and *focusing on* the good stuff is the key. When you pay attention to these good parts of your reality, your faith that more good things will happen grows stronger and stronger. Your faith in the "upside" eventually becomes a belief that lots of *good things* are going to happen — and they do. You may even start to believe that you are truly being cared for by a positive and loving universe.

You can call this power for good God, Nature, Higher Power, Love, or whatever name you like. The important thing is that you begin to have faith in the upside, faith that your world is basically a pretty good place and can even get better. Then, you can risk letting go of some of your problems and trust that this power for good in your life will, in the end, take care of things.

(SEE☞ "Serious Junkie")

You have a choice about how to look at your life, about whether you look for and see the upside or the downside. But remember, without at least a *little* faith that there is some positive force in life, the world can become a very scary place.

I'm not into isms and asms. There isn't a Catholic moon and a Baptist sun. I know the universal God is universal . . . I feel that the same God-force that is the mother and father of the pope is also the mother and father of the loneliest wino on the planet.
—Dick Gregory

Do You Believe There Is a Higher Power or Positive Force for Good in the Universe?

"No, because nothing has ever been able to prove to me that there is one, and I have grown up without ever having a specific religious faith and have done just fine, so I guess I don't need to believe."
— Lynn, 18

"Yes, I believe that when people die, they watch over you. I feel that because when my friend died I never felt so awful in my life. The next night there were lightning flashes over the accident site and I felt like she was there. I also felt her say good-bye to me. After the funeral there was a rainbow and I think it was my friend smiling and helping me out. I still feel her with me at certain times." — Ann, 18

"Yes, I believe a God created everything for a purpose. Whatever doesn't kill you makes you stronger."
— Ralph, 17

"No, I don't. I believe that we each have control over whether our lives are positive or negative. I do believe in a God, but I believe he is just a divine sort of Dear Abby who can listen and advise and then lets us make our own decisions. I suppose that could be considered a powerful force for good because I think he always wants us to do what would be best." — Michelle, 16

PERFECK-SHUNISM

Trying to be perfect is a prescription for failure. It's a way to feel constantly inadequate, incompetent, and wind up with zero self-esteem. Never being able to let go of a project because it's not done, never being able to accept your looks, your clothes, your friends, or yourself as good enough is a terrible way to go through life.

Perfeckshunism means always trying for the ultimate, absolute best that's possible, the best that anyone could ever do or be. But there's a more reasonable way: learn to recognize when YOU have done the absolute best YOU can, and then be willing to let go and feel great about it. No one on earth is perfect. If you *were* capable of perfection, you would be a pretty lonely person 'cause no one could relate to you. *Doing your best and then letting go* means self-acceptance, allowing yourself to learn and grow, to make mistakes . . . in short, giving yourself permission to be human.

MY ~~PREFECT~~ LIFE
MY PERFECT ~~LYFEN~~
~~THE~~ PERFECT ~~LEEFH~~
MY PERFECT LIFE

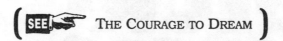

(SEE  THE COURAGE TO DREAM)

If you have trouble knowing when it's time to let go, talk it over with someone you trust. Occasionally, we all need the objective opinion and support of others.

If you are perfeckshunistic, letting go will feel risky at first. But with a willingness to learn, objectivity and support from parents, teachers, and friends — and a little practice — you'll soon find yourself more willing to be a regular person . . . doing your best.

(SEE  WEAVING A SAFETY NET)

Sit loosely in the saddle of life.

—Robert Louis Stevenson

**" *Learn to recognize when YOU* "
have done the absolute best
YOU can, and then feel great
*about it.***

What Is the Effect of Being Too Perfeck-shunistic?

"Dangerous, because if nothing feels good enough to a person, that's the main axis of low self-esteem. I feel pretty good about who I am, but I really feel like a lardass. I'm not fat, I'm just fifteen pounds too heavy, and it drives me up the wall."
— Red, 17

"Bad, because if you fail at a certain TASK, then it can make you feel as if YOU are a failure. I feel that failure is success inside out." — Jackie, 15

"Fortunately, I've found a way to fight it. When I find myself focusing on failure, filled with anxiety, I stop for a moment and remind myself of the truth. I do not become a failure because of one or any number of mistakes. I remind myself of all my successes, and by doing so, I crush the voice that lies to me by saying (things like) 'Stupid me, look, I blew it again,' or 'I can't do anything right.' "
— Steve, 17

"Some of my best friends are models. It makes me look at all the things I don't like about myself — my nose, my skin, my body's too short and a little too chunky or wide. Wanting to be perfect can drop your self-esteem to zero. When you look at yourself that way, nothing seems good enough and others are always better." — Jody, 14

"It's devastating. People set goals too high, they then can't reach them and get even more discouraged and frustrated."
— Jesse, 17

Being Loved for Breathing

We live in a competitive world that rewards the "winners" — and that leaves lots and lots of "losers." If we don't have great grades, aren't on the team, don't have a date for the dance, don't have the right clothes, or aren't skinny, we can feel like we are less than complete people. The truth is that these are NOT very healthy standards for figuring out your real worth or potential.

In our families, we can sometimes feel unloved or unlovable unless we're always doing a really great job at *something*. If situations that bring out this feeling happen often enough, our self-esteem eventually gets attached to how well we do or how we look. We then find ourselves striving to do everything perfectly, but remaining unable to accept our efforts as good enough. Just because we didn't do some *thing* well, we end up feeling not only that our work's never good enough, but that we're a failure AS A PERSON TOO. NOT TRUE!

IF WHAT YOU DO NEVER FEELS GOOD ENOUGH — OR IF YOU FEEL *YOU'RE* NEVER GOOD ENOUGH:

• Find friends who like you for who you are, who care about you NO MATTER WHAT.

• Learn how to tell the difference between doing your best and overdoing it. If this is difficult, check it out with your friends.

• Do stuff just because it makes you happy, things without measurable results: watch a sunset, listen to music, go for a walk in the woods, visit every store at the mall within an hour, read a funny book, jump in a mud puddle — you get the idea!

What Makes You Really Happy?

- "I'm happy skiing because I love the thrill; the same goes for my motorcycle." — Jesse, 17

- "Bus trips alone far away from town, taking pictures of things that are funny or pretty. I like to use my camera to take pictures of people's feelings. I love music and my guitar." — Barry, 17

- "Spending a day away from everything helps me relax and get a better perspective on life." — Marie, 14

- "Helping other people, because I feel like I'm doing something important." — Nick, 14

- "Being a gentleman, because I'm very romantic." — Wally, 17

- "Laughing and having good times with a group of close friends, no pressure and it's fun." — Delia, 16

- "Dancing, and soft furry kittens." — C. C., 14

- "Getting phone calls, and writing and receiving letters from my friends." — Jessica, 15

- "When people say I am pretty and smart because I think I am ugly and stupid." — Jody, 14

- "Working, because I LOVE money." — Jackie, 17

- "Women because I'm a man." — Chris, 17

FEELING DIFFERENT AND ALONE

Because most of us have trouble sharing the embarrassing or shameful stuff about our lives, we tend to live with secrets. As a result, we may feel that no one has a life like ours, and that at a really basic level we are different and probably less wonderful than others. We can look like others, go to the same classes, hang out in the same places, but as long as we have secrets we will feel different — and alone with those differences.

People who are down on themselves have a hard time feeling accepted, worthwhile, lovable, and deserving of the good stuff everyone else gets. It's like there's this little cloud that follows them around and casts a dark shadow over their life.

Basically we *are* all different, which is great because life would be incredibly boring if we were all the same. In fact, it's our differences that make us interesting. It means that each of

us can enrich our relationships by bringing our special gifts to them. To really enjoy our specialness, though, means we have to get past our feelings of shame and embarrassment. We have to let the sun shine through the cloud into our dark places.

(SEE 👉 TOTALLY LOVABLE)

To let go of our secret lives, we must find people we trust, and then take the risk of letting them know who we really are inside. When we do this, we most often find out how very much alike we really are, that others have had similar thoughts or have done similar things. Sharing in this way relieves us of the burden of keeping our secrets, builds trust among our friends, and frees us to enjoy ourselves and our lives more. Sharing frees us to enjoy our wonderful specialness with everyone.

If there are two hundred people in a room and one of them doesn't like me, I've got to get out.

—Marlon Brando

❝ When we let go of our secret ❞ lives, we often find out how very much alike we really are.

What Would You Tell a Young Person Who Was Feeling Different?

● "I'd tell them they're not different, that they're just like everyone else. Not having money or stylish clothes means nothing. What counts is how you feel about you."— Shelli, 14

● "Things will change. There are a MILLION other young people who feel the same way."
— Jessica, 15

● "That you are unique and not to feel down on yourself, but to feel proud that you're different and unique. Be yourself and don't try to act and look phony."
— John, 16

● "Cheer up, I used to feel the same way, but as times change so do people." — Jesse, 17

● "I would tell them that we ARE all different, but in a lot of ways we're the same. We all go through more or less the same things and we're all human."
— Marie, 14

● "That it's beautiful to be yourself and sometimes people aren't open if you're not like them, but just be you anyway." — Elle, 17

● "You are never an outsider if you're an insider in your own life. Like what you've got."
— Chris, 17

● "I'd tell 'em they're lucky because chances are they are the ones who have it all together." — Delia, 16

Totally Lovable

You were born wonderful, mostly happy and full of love. If you don't think you're lovable now, it's because you got confused along the way. Sometimes we learn from others that we are worthy of love *only* if we meet certain conditions. We get fooled into thinking we have to *do* something or *be* something or *have* something to be loved and accepted. This is a **BIG** misconception.

If you believe you have to meet certain conditions before you can feel good about yourself, you are contributing to your own low self-esteem. Learning unconditional *self*-love and *self*-acceptance is a big part of having strong self-esteem.

 (SEE ☞ GETTING A NEW COACH)

If you believe you have to live up to the expectations of *others* before you are worthy of their love and acceptance, you are giving people power over you. You're letting them determine YOUR self-worth. People who withhold love or acceptance till you do it their way are just blackmailing you.

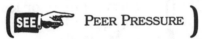 (SEE ☞ PEER PRESSURE)

UNCONDITIONAL SELF-LOVE means really believing that **NO MATTER WHAT** other people think of me, I AM A WONDERFUL, LOVABLE PERSON!

If you don't believe that is true, talk to your friends for an objective view. If that doesn't help, consider counseling or a support group. Feeling totally lovable is point zero, the place you *have to* start. From there, you can find people who accept and like you for who you are.

 (SEE ☞ HAVING FRIENDS AND WEAVING A SAFETY NET)

They will respond to *your* belief that:

RIGHT NOW, NO MATTER WHAT I HAVE BEEN TAUGHT TO FEEL ABOUT MYSELF, I LOVE AND RESPECT MYSELF TOTALLY.

- "Yes sir-ree, Bob!" — Rebecca, 16
- "Yes, I think so, to a point." — Maggie, 15
- "When I want to be." — Mary, 18
- "No." — John, 17
- "Sometimes." — Jenny, 17
- "I try to be." — Kerry, 16

Are You a Wonderful and Lovable Person?

"*If-ing*" Yourself

Sometimes we "if only" ourselves out of feeling good about who we are. Here is a list of just some of the possible barriers to really loving yourself. See how many "if only's" stand in the way of YOU loving yourself unconditionally.

I will love myself if only:

I win	I perform well	I am smart
I have a boyfriend	Others like me	I am happy
I am healthy	I have money	I look good
I have a girlfriend	I am funny	People call me
I am cool	I am right	I don't cry
I have a lot of friends	I get my way	I have it all
I get great grades	I am not afraid	together

When we live with so many self-imposed barriers, it's a wonder we can like ourselves at all! That is why we need each other's love and support.

(concept by Gary Legwold, 1990)

97

I Love Myself The Way I Am

I love myself the way I am,
there's nothing I need to change.
I'll always be the perfect me,
there's nothing to rearrange.
I'm beautiful and capable of being
the best me I can,
and I love myself just the way I am.

I love you just the way you are,
there's nothing you need to do.
When I feel the love inside myself,
it's easy to love you.

Behind your fears, your rage and
tears,
I see your shining star.
And I love you just the way you
are.

I love the world the way it is,
'cause I can clearly see,
that all the things I judge are done
by people just like me.

So till the birth of peace on earth,
that only love can bring,
I'll help it grow by loving
everything.

I love myself the way I am
and still I want to grow.
The change outside can only
 come
when deep inside I know,
I'm beautiful and capable of
being
the best me I can.
And I love myself just the way I
am.

I love myself just the way I am.

Lyrics by Jai Josefs. © 1990
Jai-Jo Music (BMI)
All rights reserved. Used with
permission.

Self-Esteem Assessment

For each of the words on this page, think back until you remember a time you showed this quality. Give yourself 100 points for each item you can remember. Don't give up until you come up with an example for each one. Add up your points when you're done. Anyone scoring 1500 points is a truly fine human being. Anyone scoring less than 1500 is a truly fine human being with a terrible memory!

Determined	Gentle	Funny
Friendly	Generous	Loyal
Grateful	Helpful	Inventive
Honest	Good listener	Patient
Responsible	Sensitive	Kind

"The thing I like best about myself is that I'm me and nobody else."

— Kate, 11

98

What Is Self-Esteem, And How Can You Tell If Someone Doesn't Have It?

● "Self-esteem is the feelings and emotions that you have about yourself. It colors how you look at yourself and how you look at others. People with low self-esteem will look at the negative side of people and things and criticize everything." — Elyse, 17

● "Self-esteem is how secure you are. It's how strongly you trust your abilities and how content you are with yourself. It's how adept you are at accepting yourself and making the absolute most out of what you have." — Michelle, 16

● "People without self-esteem put others down or take their problems out on others. They want to hurt people because it will somehow make them feel better about themselves." — Mary, 18

● "Self-esteem is about how you view yourself as a person. People without it keep putting themselves down and say stuff like, 'I can't do anything right,' and 'I'm so dumb.' " — Debra, 15

● "To think you can do things, to try and not quit, believing you can accomplish something." — Nicole, 15

● "Everyone has self-esteem, some people's just isn't as high as others. If they have bad self-esteem they are shy and drawn back from people." — Missy, 16

What Can You Do to Improve Your Self-Esteem or That of Others?

● "Get friends who like you for you and not your brand of jeans. Look at yourself in the mirror and say good things over and over until you believe them. I say, 'I am a worthwhile person and I deserve to be loved.' Try not to beat yourself up if you don't do things perfect. Accept that making mistakes makes you human." — Lynn, 18

● "You can help your friends with encouragement, support, and liking them for who they are. Respect them and care for them. Help them when they have problems or give advice if they ask for it. Don't think about the little things they do that irritate you. Tell them they are a good person and you like being around them. That you're glad they're your friend." — Mary, 18

● "Assure myself that I'm important and just because I can't do one thing doesn't mean I can't do anything else." — Kirstin, 15

● "Don't listen to people that put you down." — Missy, 16

● "Write in a journal about the positive in my day, remember the compliments I got, and maintain my food diary." — Sara, 17

● "You can improve your friends' self-esteem when you compliment them if they deserve it. Tell them you love them and they're wonderful, don't just assume they know. Be there when they need you." — Joe, 16

SAY WHAT?

What is vaginismus? . . . How can I get the boy in biology class to notice me?. . . What is a transsexual? . . . Can you pass sexual warts on to your child?. . . Can you get pregnant from oral sex?. . . What is the cause of sterility?. . . What is impotence?. . . Can you catch AIDS from kissing?

—Questions asked in Social Living class at Berkeley High as reported in Life, July 1989

Today, sex can do more than paralyze teenagers with anxiety; it can kill them. Teenagers comprise 0.4 percent of all AIDS patients; they also have the highest rate of other sexually-transmitted diseases (STDs), from chlamydia to venereal warts to herpes. The U.S. has the highest teen birthrate in the Western world. More than half of all

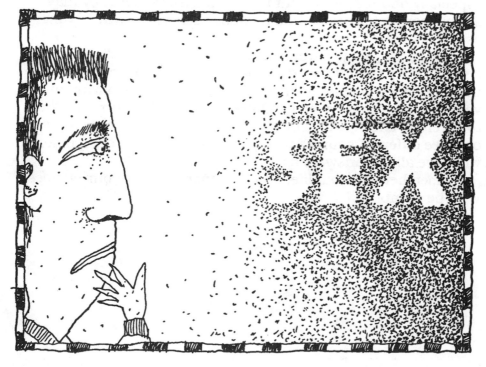

teenagers have had intercourse by the age of 17; less than half use contraception on a regular basis. Bombarded by sexual messages in the media, in music, and on TV, how do they make their decisions?

—*Life, July 1989, p. 24*

You Need to Know

If you know enough to have questions about sex, you deserve some straight answers. Without straight answers about sex, you can make mistakes that can harm you and somebody else, sometimes for life. Good information is available. Make sure the answers you get are right before you base your decisions about sex on them.

 (SEE☞ PEER PRESSURE)

Going to your parents first can be a very good idea if you feel comfortable talking with them about the subject. Sometimes it is very hard for parents, however, to know how to approach the subject of sex with you. Some parents weren't taught very much about sexuality while they were growing up, and as a result, they don't have very good answers themselves — especially about more recent issues like AIDS. Or they may simply have a hard time talking about sexuality with anyone — especially their kids.

Trust and try your parents first, but if that doesn't work, go elsewhere for the information you need. A school counselor or health science teacher, your local public health department, or your family doctor are all good places to start. Just remember to carefully check things out. You may even want to go to two or three different sources with your questions. No one person will have all the answers for you.

Remember, it's *your* life. *You're* responsible for your choices. Why be dumb!

 (SEE☞ WEAVING A SAFETY NET)

What Is the Most Confusing, Frightening, or Positive Aspect About Sexuality for You?

What Would You Say to Other Young People About Sexuality?

● "If you don't understand sex and what can happen from it, such as AIDS and pregnancy, you could end up dead or with a family at a very young age. Your life could be a lot happier and safer if you ask questions."
— Kristi, 15

● "Confusing — knowing how far to let guys go. Frightening — wondering if you're too 'flat'. I would tell young people that before you have sex, know yourself and your body first. If you have any questions, talk to somebody about them."
— Jody, 14

● "The most confusing aspect of sexuality for me is knowing when it's the right time for sex. You might think you're ready and mature enough to handle it, but afterwards you realize you weren't. The most frightening aspect is pregnancy. The responsibility and social effects are too overwhelming for someone my age." — Nick, 14

● "I think it is great, but I also think that it can get to be a problem for some people. For me, it became an addiction, a way too important a part of my relationships." — Steven, 17

● "I don't understand why sex has to be the ultimate show of love and affection." — Jesse, 17

● "I am frightened that I might catch some kind of disease, and I'm grossed out when I think about all the other girls this guy may have been with."
— Loretta, 15

What Do You Feel Adults Just Don't Understand About the Problems Kids Have in Dealing with Sexuality?

● "It is like adults forgot what it was like. They were kids once too; times don't change that fast!" — Jesse, 17

● "How can they expect their kids to not be interested in sex when music, TV, movies, and even the telephones are almost 'exploding' with sex."
— A. C., 17

● "I think when adults try to ignore the issue they are not only hurting themselves, but the kids as well. Kids are going to do it and they should be informed about birth control."
— Steven, 17

● "I guess the main thing is that adults don't realize that sex is a very real thing to us, and not as easy to abstain from as adults seem to think." — Nick, 14

● "A lot of kids have sex like it was just a leisure activity like bingo or skiing. Kids mostly have casual sex that doesn't mean anything. I think this 'kids have loose morals' thing is blown tremendously out of proportion. People should wonder about morals when they pollute the planet, drink alcohol, and don't vote." — Wally, 17

WHY KIDS STEAL

It's very weird to be a basically honest person who all of a sudden, out of the blue, just steals something. More often than not, we take things we don't even need or want. We don't see ourselves as a thief. And yet, that's what we are. Stealing is stealing, and it's never ok. So why do we do it? Perhaps one or more of the following factors are affecting us:

- **"All my friends do it!"** — Some of us need to be accepted by others so badly, we'll do whatever it takes to gain others' approval.

(SEE ☞ PEER PRESSURE)

- **To feel competent** — If we aren't doing very well at some of the things our family or school values — like clean rooms, good grades, or athletic ability, for instance, we may not feel

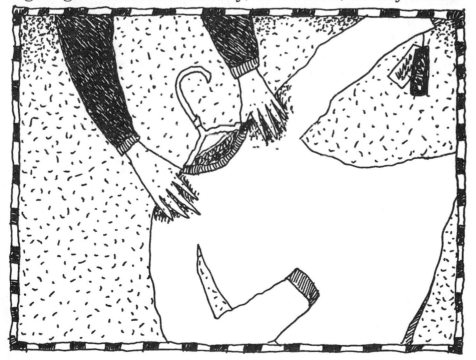

very good at anything we do. Stealing something and not getting caught gives us a sense of accomplishment and skill.

(SEE ☞ TOTALLY LOVABLE)

- **For adventure** — Some of us are totally bored with life. We're looking for a little adventure, or some excitement. Anything for a rush.

(SEE ☞ THE COURAGE TO DREAM)

- **To get things** — Some families either can't afford or just won't buy even the inexpensive things their kids want. So some kids just take things because they want them.

- **To get even** — Some of us are full of anger. We may not even remember who or what we're angry about — we've just become angry people. Stealing can become a way to get even, a kind of "I'll show them" behavior.

(SEE ☞ THE HUMAN VOLCANO)

We all have healthy needs for acceptance, excitement, challenge, self-worth, and expressing our feelings. Stealing is just an illegal, wasteful, and stupid way to go about meeting these needs. The important question to ask yourself is *not* how to steal without getting caught — but what *real* needs are we trying to meet and *how do we get them met in a positive way?* No matter how "good" we are at theft, we won't feel good inside in the long run. We'll never hurt a store, the school, or a parent as much as we'll hurt ourselves.

Why Do You Think Young People Steal?

● "It's a challenge. It's got this hard-to-explain thrill to it, and it fights boredom." — Delia, 16

● "If you have been a 'good' kid all your life, you get sick of being so good. So you'll do lots of stuff to prove you can be bad."
— Jody, 14

● "To prove they can get by the system. Kids feel invincible when they think they have beat a system run by a group of adults." — Nick, 14

● "To get attention from their friends and to prove that they aren't afraid of anyone."
— Loretta, 15

● "I think they shoplift because they want the attention they don't get at home. Even if they don't want to admit it, they want their parents' attention."
— Marie, 14

● "The adventure, the excitement, the challenge." — Jesse, 17

WHAT IS STRESS?

Imagine that you were a strange sort of person who, whenever you came across a rubber band, you put it around your head. Some rubber bands would be big and fat and others small and thin, but on and on they'd go, one on top of another. Before long, your head would resemble a weird, giant rubber ball . . . and the pressure on your brain would be tremendous.

Stress can slowly build up in us like this too. Imagine that each fear, problem, or worry we have is one of those rubber bands. Some are big and others small, but each contributes nevertheless to our overall discomfort. Because our worries and fears come to us gradually, over time, we usually don't realize they are piling up. But as they do, we just unconsciously adapt to more and more pressure, while at the same time trying to function normally — like we always have.

As the pressure builds, a number of things can happen. Just like we wouldn't feel

each of those rubber bands individually, we don't feel and experience every individual fear or worry, either. But when we get enough of those worry, fear, and pressure "rubber bands" wrapped around us, we sense there's a major danger out there somewhere — though we just can't say where. Instead, we become GENERALLY more anxious and fearful—

(**SEE** ☞ WORRY)

and we tend to be more on guard with *everything*. Like a cat or dog in an unfamiliar neighborhood, we're always nervous and on the lookout for problems or danger.

Keeping our guard up all the time puts an enormous strain on our whole body — it's a lot of work. Eventually our body complains and begins to send out signals that something is very wrong.

(**SEE** ☞ THE PHYSICAL SIDE OF STRESS)

In addition to physical problems showing up, our good attitude begins to wear thin too. With less energy, enthusiasm, patience, and good humor, we can no longer function at our best. Because we don't feel good anymore and life seems generally pretty scary, we're likely to withdraw more and more from the world.

(**SEE** ☞ DEALING WITH THE FEELING)

Unfortunately, that choice takes us away from what we need the most, like support and love. So this circle gets tighter and tighter: we feel worse, withdraw more, and down we go in an ever-increasing negative spiral.

The better choice? Get rid of the old "rubber bands" of stress, and then stop adding new ones.

(**SEE** ☞ PROBLEM MANAGEMENT)

Hot Quotes on Stress

"Stress is like . . . your body is full of little angry guys inside you." — Gary, 15

"The way I normally deal with stress is by keeping all my feelings inside, but I'm trying to reach out to others and ask for support. I really don't think that there's much we can do to relieve stress because it's always going to be there in one form or another." — Dorene, 15

"Kids don't use drugs to be cool. That faded out a few years ago. Now kids are mistakenly thinking drugs help them deal with the stress of life." — Paula, 18

"Stay a kid as long as you can because it doesn't get easier." — Ryan, 15

"Adults can relieve some stress. They can stop putting so much pressure on us to excel and limit themselves to encouraging us, so when we do something, we'll have done it for us, not for them!" — Jennifer, 14

Dealing With The Feeling

It's not fun to feel stressed out, and it's natural for people to want to escape feelings of pressure and discomfort. Any means a person uses to avoid stressful FEELINGS is called short-term coping. Why "short" term? Because it only works for a little while. Whenever we stop our escape attempts, our life is there again, just waiting with the same stressful feelings. There's no place, no way, to hide from them for long. The old saying is really true: "Wherever you go, there you are." We just can't get away from ourselves for very long.

Unfortunately, no matter what method we choose to escape from feeling bad, IT DOESN'T FIX THE PROBLEM.

(**SEE** ☞ WAYS TO ESCAPE FEELINGS)

So while we are busy escaping, our problems remain unsolved and are probably getting worse. We create a crazy circle for ourselves: the more we run away from our feelings, the worse our problems get, and the more we feel the need to run away. As a result, we increase the amount we drink, eat, smoke, gamble, work, study, have sex, or *whatever* it is we're doing to not feel the ever-increasing pressure.

As the cycle continues, our behavior can get pretty weird and even self-destructive. As the pressure builds and our life gets worse, we usually find it necessary to lie to cover up our escape behavior. Some of us get so good at lying about our behavior and do it so often that we can't tell what's true for ourselves any more. When we don't know how bad our life has gotten because of all the escape behaviors we're using, it's called *denial.*

When we continue to use escape behaviors in spite of harmful consequences, we could have a serious problem — a behavior disorder or addiction — that needs outside help. Unless we get help and really start looking at what we're doing, over time stress, denial, and the need to escape will continue to increase. This can go on a long time — usually until something in our life goes *very* wrong.

Not everybody becomes addicted to a substance or a behavior to deal with stress. Some of us, however, just seem to be made in such a way that alcohol, other drugs, and mood-altering behaviors trigger an addictive cycle. When this happens, we need major help. Fortunately, there are lots of self-help groups to turn to when things are tough. If you sense that you MIGHT be caught in a destructive coping cycle, **reach out for help.** There are better ways to deal with feeling bad, and the price you are paying is way too high.

God grant me the serenity
to accept the things I cannot change,
the courage to change the things I can,
and the wisdom to know the difference.

—Reinhold Niebuhr
The Serenity Prayer

Problem Management

Problem management means recognizing, working through, and getting rid of as many old fears, worries, and pressures as you can — and then trying not to add new ones.

The ultimate goal is to see and deal with your stress-makers as soon as possible after they appear. If you do this, you can pretty much keep stress-caused pressures from building up in you at all. Here are a few things you can do to reduce the stress you feel:

Make a List of Your Stress-Makers

It is helpful to be aware of the things in your life that cause you stress. Writing them down on paper can help you see your problems more clearly and even reduce some of their power over you. Your feelings won't be so vague or mysterious, and you'll have a better idea how to take positive action.

Sorting It All Out

On your list of problems, fears, concerns, and pressures, you'll find some things you can do something about, and others that remain out of your control. Once you know which is which, you won't need to put too much energy into the ones you can't do anything about. Look at the ones you think you *can* work with, and then decide which ones deserve attention first.

Start Small

At first, pick some of the little things. They will be easier to handle, and besides, it's nice to have a few early successes at making a positive difference in your life. It helps you build up the courage to tackle the bigger issues.

Get Support

When you have problems, the most important action you can take is to talk to someone you trust. Because you are so involved with your problems, you just can't be really clear and objective about what to do. And talking to someone you trust about what is making you afraid, confused, or ashamed is the best way to reduce the uncomfortable feelings.

Getting your feelings and problems out in the open, feeling cared about by friends, hearing an objective viewpoint, or just

113

learning you are not alone with your concerns — these are just some of the benefits that can come from sharing your fears and worries.

(SEE ☞ PEOPLE I CAN TRUST AND WEAVING A SAFETY NET)

Imagine you'd been putting stress "rubber bands" around your head for fifteen years — one for every worry and problem and fear you'd had and kept inside. Imagine how good it would feel to have those old rubber bands gradually removed. Imagine getting so healthy and skilled at handling problems and feelings as they come up that you never put another one on your head. Imagine having ten trustworthy friends you could call whenever you felt a little stressed out. That is what problem management is like, *once you begin tackling your problems as they come up.*

What Makes You Stressed Out?

Family:

● "My parents have divorced and remarried. I get moved back and forth every other weekend. With new kids in my house there isn't enough time for everyone so I feel left out."
— Debra, 14

● "The pressure from family to succeed, and them always asking why I'm not more like my brother." — Michelle, 16

● "Parents constantly arguing and my mother always on my back about something." — Ann, 18

● "My dad's girlfriend always yelling at me for stupid reasons." — Marie, 16

● "It drives me nuts when my mom always interrupts me when I'm trying to talk to her."
— Kirstin, 15

School:

● "Rumors, two-faced people, materialism, and male chauvinist teachers!" — Sara, 17

● "With the way I was brought up, school is more important than anything; I live for grades and hate myself for it." — Debra, 16

● "Sometimes I feel I can't handle it and there are times I'd like to say 'forget it' but I don't."
— Mary, 18

● "Peers shunning me because I don't dress the same as they do or hang out with the 'right' crowd." — Michelle, 16

● "Grades, people who don't even know your first name but judge you anyway, rumors."
— Ann, 18

What Makes You Stressed Out?

Friends:

- "When my friends are making choices I know are only leading to trouble, or when they're going through tough times and I can't do anything to help."
— Michelle, 16

- "Dealing with my friends' problems 'cause I'm the type of person that absorbs everyone else's problems."
— Lynn, 18

- "Sometimes they push you to be something you're not. My friends are great, but they're not perfect."
— Mary, 18

- "When friends let you down."
— Ann, 18

- "I've got a few but I always wonder if they truly are my friends."
— John, 17

- "When I am running around fixing everyone's problems."
— Leigh, 13

Life in General:

- "Sometimes everything comes down on me at once and I feel like I'm going insane."
— Mary, 18

- "Trying to be popular, skinny, and feeling like an outcast compared to others." — Sara, 17

- "It's not very much fun. Trying to make everyone happy, school, chores, family matters. It's too hard. I didn't have much of a childhood."
— Debra, 16

- "When I don't do as well as I know I could or when I have a lot of things happening all at once, good or bad."
— Michelle, 16

What Things Do You Do To Feel Better When You Are Totally Stressed Out?

● "Sleep, relax with my dog, go down by the river with a friend, or sometimes just scream." — Ann, 18

● "Not much — I try not to lay my crap on my friends because they have enough to deal with on their own. So I am filled up most of the time and my body reacts with rashes and chronic bronchitis." — Lynn, 18

● "I listen to the radio and clean my room. When I am in the mood, I write poems or paint. Other times I just sit in my room and cry." — Debra, 16

● "Heavy exercise takes my mind off of things, and when I go back to my problems I find it easier to put things in perspective. I talk to other people and find out what they did in similar situations. Sometimes all I need is a good cry before I dive back in and sort things out. But no matter what, eventually I have to deal with things and not run away." — Michelle, 16

● "Punch a pillow or locker. Scream or cry." — Devon, 17

● "After exercising I feel so energized and relaxed." — Elyse, 17

● "I listen to music, play my piano or dance." — Kirstin, 15

● "I just read or talk to a friend or just go sit and think for a while." — Leigh, 13

The Physical Side of Stress

All humans — even your marginally human friends — have a common physical response to feeling stressed out. It is called the *Fight or Flight Response*. Very simply put, in moments of PERCEIVED danger, your body gets ready to fight or run. (The key here is **perceived** danger — but more on that in a bit!) We have a special nervous system whose main job is to keep us alive by doing battle with or getting us away from things that threaten us. Here is a list of SOME of the things that your body does every time you are fearful:

- **Your breathing gets faster**: This change makes more oxygen available to the bloodstream for energy and top performance.

- **Your heart beats faster**: To get oxygen-rich blood to the brain and muscles as quickly as possible.

- **The big arteries in your neck open wide**: This allows blood to flow to your brain quicker. It may make your face look pink and feel warm, your ears hot, or give you a "pressure" headache. It can also make you feel dizzy or light-headed.

- **The small blood vessels in your hands and feet contract**: When these vessels get smaller, blood flow to your hands and feet is restricted. This change makes more blood available to big muscles in your arms, legs, back, and abdomen for running and fighting. This change can also make your hands and feet cold.

- **Your body sweats**: Sweating is how the body cools off. Because running and fighting generate a lot of heat, the body starts its cooling process right away. This may cause your hands and feet to get damp.

- **Your digestive tract shuts down**: The body can't be bothered with processing lunch when you life is at risk, so the digestive system shuts down. This change also makes more blood available elsewhere in your body. Your mouth may get really dry or your stomach may feel upset.

- **Your glands and organs release chemicals**: Every gland and organ has a special function during the fight-or-flight response, and they all get in gear to help "save" you. The one you're probably most familiar with is adrenalin — it causes the feeling of "butterflies" in your stomach.

118

While some of these responses may make you think you're sick, they're actually signs that your body is healthy and working as it should.

No matter what the threat, our body's response to it is the same — only the intensity varies, and that's based on our PERCEPTION of how much danger we're really in. Just thinking about a scary situation — or even watching a scary movie, for example — sets off the fight-or-flight response. Our body can't tell the difference between a "real" dangerous situation and one only created in our head by our worries. The fight-or-flight response is designed for "emergency use only." But if you worry a lot, your body will be in this revved-up state often. Maintaining the fight-or-flight state is really hard on your body, and really exhausting too.

( WORRY)

What Physical And Emotional Signals Do You Get When You Are Really Stressed Out?

- "Physically, I get headaches, stomachaches, and sometimes dizziness. Emotionally, I get very cold towards people and often will blow up at them for no reason. Sometimes I just cry for no reason too." — Nick, 14

- "Sometimes I actually get shaky. I get a ton of anxiety and feel like things are out of control." — Steve, 18

- "I can feel the tension building up in my body and sometimes I get a headache. I get mad very easy and cry more often." — Shelli, 14

- "I get shaky and nervous, lock my breath up inside so I have to take deep breaths. I get angry, frustrated, and my thoughts start racing." — Al, 17

- "My pace slows down and I can't concentrate, I daydream more. I get really depressed and moody. All I wanna do is put on my *Phantom of the Opera* tape and lay in the bathtub." — Loretta, 15

- "I get major breakouts of zits, I am really tired and I get bags under my eyes. When I'm stressed out I want to cry about everything." — Jody, 14

WEAVING A SAFETY NET

We are all in this alone . . . together.

—Anonymous

I can still remember watching the high wire act at the circus when I was a kid. What tremendous courage it took to fly through the air so high off the ground. Each moment I was afraid that one slip might result in disaster. It wasn't till the end of their act, when the performers would fly and spin through spectacular dismounts into the net below that I realized they really had been safe the whole time — that, in fact, the net had **allowed them** to take those risks.

I can't imagine why anyone would want to take big risks without a safety net. Yet when we are going through change in

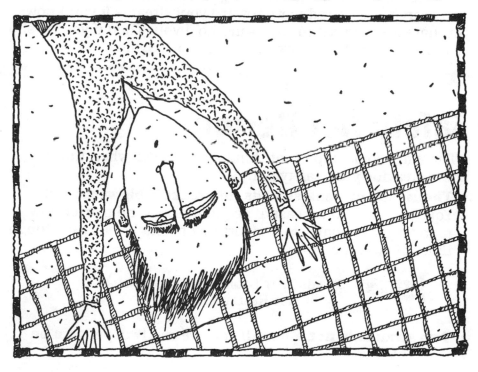

our life, experiencing a loss, or trying something new, many of us still try to get by without a safety net of human support.

We often get the message that we should be able to handle everything ourselves, that we shouldn't ask for help when we are hurting, or that we shouldn't trust other people. Yet without a number of reliable people for support in our lives, we will be like a trapeze artist *without* a net. Risks that are reasonable with a "human safety net" may become much greater without one, and increase our chances of really being hurt or falling into fear and hopelessness.

You can weave your safety net by developing relationships with people you trust.

(**SEE** ☞ PEOPLE I CAN TRUST)

Make the strongest strands out of parents and relatives, reliable friends, people who share your spiritual beliefs, and some teachers, counselors, or other trustworthy adults. Around these strands, you can weave the others — those who like the same sports, hobbies, music, or other activities, or just people who make you laugh.

If you are living through an especially difficult period of your life, the people who make up your net will be there to comfort and encourage you. They can keep you focused on your strengths, and keep you from falling into fear, negativity, or low self-esteem. You'll be more willing to take the risks that are necessary to grow and move toward your dreams if you know you have a safety net to catch and hold you. Then if you do slip or fall, you can climb back up and go for it again.

Safety Net Design

There are some important things to consider when thinking about weaving your safety net.

- **Thousands of weak strands just make a big weak net.**
  You need more than casual acquaintances, no matter how many you may have, to support you through the really tough times of your life.

(**SEE** ☞ THINGS THAT LOOK LIKE FRIENDSHIP BUT REALLY AREN'T)

- **Two strands is not a net.** If you are overly dependent on one or two people, like a parent, or a boyfriend or girlfriend, you'll be pretty vulnerable if they can't be there for you when you really need them.

(SEE 👉 HAVING FRIENDS)

- **Your net gets stronger the more you use it!** Unlike other safety nets, human safety nets increase in strength and value the more you use them. Trust that other people's ability and willingness to be there for you will grow as you use them for support. And the more you trust them, the more you'll become willing to take bigger risks because you know your net is there for you — strong and secure.

66 *Without reliable people in our* **99**
lives for support, we're like a
trapeze artist without a net.

PEOPLE I CAN TRUST

Having trustworthy people in our life is vital. They don't always have to be our best friends. They can be any person we feel safe with or have learned to trust over time — a teacher, counselor, friend, parent, relative, or neighbor.

Unfortunately, these people don't usually just appear in our lives. Such relationships most often have to be built up over time. If you know what to look for, though, you can find good candidates and begin to develop relationships built on trust.

Here are a few traits of trustworthy people:

- **Great listeners:** They don't try to fix your problems or give uninvited advice; they just listen and communicate their understanding and support.

- **Non-critical:** They don't judge you; they accept you for who you are.

- **Keep secrets**: You can share your worst fears, concerns, and joys without worrying that they will pass them around.

- **Reliable:** They can be counted on to be on time, to do what they say they will do, and to offer help when you need it.

- **Consistent**: Their lives are pretty steady, with no huge ups and downs — they aren't friends one day and enemies the next.

- **Can see the upside**: They can help you stay in touch with what is wonderful about you and your life.

- **Honest**: They'll tell you the truth — about how they feel and how they see you.

Why Is It Important to Have People In Your Life That You Can Really Trust?

Describe a Time When You Really Needed a Trustworthy Friend.

● "Because everyone has a secret or two in their life and it is really important to tell them to someone so you don't feel bad and different. When my family was having a hard time, my best friend was right by my side the whole time." — Maggie, 15

● "To know that you aren't the only person in the world with problems like yours and that there is someone who cares about you." — Lynn, 16

● "You can't keep your feelings trapped inside of you all of the time, so it is necessary to have people who can listen." — Mirella, 18

● "I don't have anyone in life that I trust so I don't know why it's important. I could use a trustworthy friend anytime because I have enough problems and secrets to need one all the time." — Catherine, 14

● "When my friend died, I needed a hand to hold. The first person I asked let me down, then I realized I had thirty more I could ask. A lot of friends laughed and cried with me, cared, listened, and shared their feelings too." — Ann, 18

● "People always have things that they need to tell someone. Like the time I finally decided to speak up about the sexual abuse when I was younger. My best friend really listened. She didn't force me into doing anything or telling anyone I didn't want to. AND she didn't judge me." — Devon, 17

THE ILLUSION OF PROGRESS

*Some of your hurts you have cured,
and some of the sharpest you've even survived,
but what torments of grief you've endured
from evils that never arrived.*

—*Ralph Waldo Emerson*

We all have things we worry about. We often become anxious and unconsciously run our worries over and over and over in our mind. If we were to pay close attention to our worrying, we would probably hear some of the same concerns come by again and again.

 SEE ☞ ELEVATOR MUSIC IN YOUR HEAD)

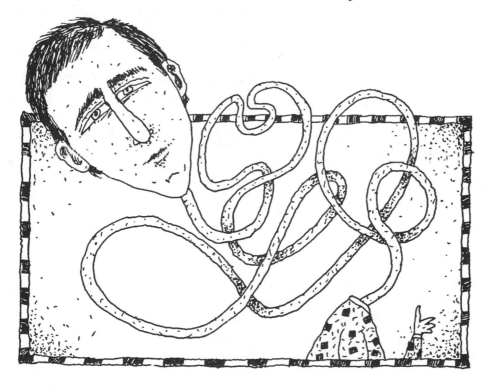

One reason we keep worrying is that worrying *itself* creates the ILLUSION that we're doing something about a problem, that we are "working" on it. The truth is, *worrying is an absolute waste of time.* Worrying is not a problem-solving activity. Worry does not give us the real support and objectivity of our friends. It does not give us a plan of action, or help us set goals for change. **Worrying simply doesn't do anything** that actually makes a positive difference in our lives.

Then just what *does* worrying do? It makes us feel afraid, stirs up our body's "fight-or-flight" response, and contributes to bad health.

(SEE ☞ THE PHYSICAL SIDE OF STRESS)

It builds a bad attitude, leads to more worry, and cheats us out of experiencing the present in a positive way.

(SEE ☞ THE ATTITUDE MAGNIFYING GLASS)

I mean, really, WHY BOTHER?

ZTIROFOG

Good-bye from **Earl and Larry**, With a **Little Help** from the **Uoyfolla Tribe**

We hope that the stuff in this book makes some difference in your life. Growth as a person often comes about through lots of little changes made gradually. So if by using this book you learn something new about yourself, believe in yourself a little more, or are more open to developing trust in relationships, or all of the above, Larry and I will be a couple of happy guys.

Life will present you with hard times and major challenges. That's why we want to leave you with the magical word "Ztirofog" to give you courage. Ztirofog — pronounced "Troh-fog" because the "z" and the "i" are silent — is sometimes

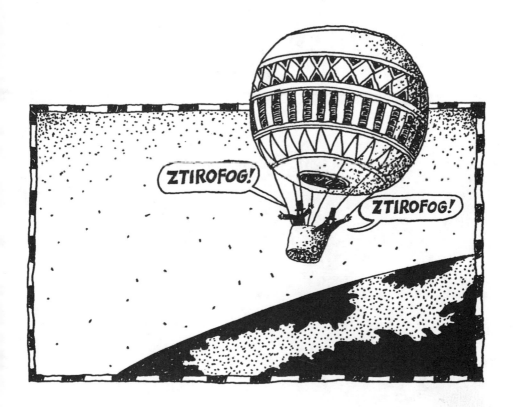

shortened further to "trow-foe." This word is a favorite expression of the happy and very smart Uoyfolla (oye-fall-a) tribe who are known for their individualism, sense of humor, creative problem-solving, risk-taking, their caring nature, ingenuity, playfulness, resourcefulness, and intense hatred of riding school buses.

"Ztirofog" has no exact equivalent in English, but roughly translated means "love yourself, take the risks that are necessary to grow, trust your ability to get through the tough times, and ask for help when you need it." Because life in the jungle is no picnic, the Uoyfolla people go around saying "Ztirofog" to each other a lot.

So our very best to you, and "Ztirofog, Ztirofog, Ztirofog!"

THE FEELINGS INDEX

WHERE IN THE BOOK TO LOOK IF YOU'RE FEELING . . .

A

accepted

totally lovable, p 96; feeling different and alone, p 93; peer pressure, p 79; belonging needs, p 80

afraid

of change, p 15; of anger, p 7; of feelings, p 37; of loss, p 51; of sex, p 101; of being alone, p 125; getting "wings," p 75; stressed-out, p 109

alone

losing someone, p 51; in crisis, p 19; escaping feelings, p 40; peer pressure, p 80; having friends, p 45; feeling alone, p 93; finding support, p 121

angry

human volcano, p 7; sideways anger, p 8; having feelings, p 37; stress and anger, p 111

annoyed

see *angry*

anxious

see *worried*

B

beautiful

perfect body, p 13; uniquely beautiful, p 14; totally lovable, p 96

bitter

sideways anger, p 8; human volcano, p 7; dealing with feelings, p 37

bored

change, p 15; having feelings, p 37; new friends, p 45

bummed out

see *depressed*

C

calm

in time of crisis, p 20; staying calm, pp 84, 111, 125; with parents, p 75; problem management, p 113

carefree

why worry, p 129; "elevator music" in your head, p 1

careful

about change, p 15; about sex, p 101; in a crisis, p 19; with drugs, p 33; on your own, p 75; trusting others, 125

cautious

see *careful*

concerned

about a friend, p 59; drug use, p 33; about your body, p 13; real friends, p 45; trust, p 125

confident

growing self-confidence, p 4; faith in the upside, p 83; courage to dream, p 27; in body image, p 13

confused

about a crisis, p 19; about change, p 15; about sex, p 101; about parents, p 75; real friends, p 45; problem management, p 113

content
totally lovable, p 96; why worry, p 129

courageous
courage to change, p 15; in crisis, p 19; peer pressure, p 79; getting "wings," p 75; trust, p 125; weaving a safety net, p 122

crabby
having feelings, p 37; anger, pp 7, 9; with parents, p 75, 77

D

defeated
stuck in the muck, p 71; depression, p 23; getting help, p 63; getting a new coach, pp 1, 4; being loved for breathing, p 90

depressed
depression, p 23; over a loss, p 51; stressed-out p 111; big trouble, p 60; over-helping friends, p 63; problem management, p 113

disappointed
courage to dream, p 27; positive universe, p 83; weaving a safety net, p 122; courage and change, p 15

discouraged
perfectionism, p 87; getting a new coach, p 4; also see *disappointed*

dumb
totally lovable, p 96; getting a new coach, p 4; stuck in the muck, p 71

E

eager
faith in the upside, p 83; courage to dream, p 27

elated
what makes you happy, p 91; getting "wings," p 75; faith in the upside, p 83

embarrassed
low self-worth, p 71; peer pressure, p 89; perfectionism, p 87

empty
grief, p 51; during changes, p 15; loss, p 51; weaving a safety net, p 122

enthusiastic
see *excited*

excited
loved for breathing, p 90; faith in the upside, p 83; dreams, p 27; why bother worrying, p 129

F

fat
body image, p 13; being loved for breathing, p 90; perfectionism, p 89; getting a new coach, p 4

frustrated
courage to dream, p 27; why worry, p 129; perfectionism, p 87; problem management, p 113; also see *disappointed*

G

glad
faith in the positive, p 84; why bother worrying, p 129; living with change, p 15; value of friendship, p 45; getting "wings," p 75

great

see *excited, eager*

guilty

low self-worth, p 71; guilt vs. shame, p 71; after a loss, p 55; totally lovable, p 96

H

handsome

totally lovable, p 96; body image, p 13

happy

see *glad*

hopeful

faith in the upside, p 83; getting "wings," p 75

hopeless

depression, p 23; getting a new coach, p 4; totally lovable, p 96; courage to change, p 15; "serious" junkie, p 26; also see *defeated*

hurt

hurting yourself with drugs, p 33; about a loss, p 51; anger, p 7; having feelings, p 37; real friends, p 50; weaving a safety net, p 122

I

inadequate

totally lovable, p 96; accepting yourself, p 90; people you can trust, p 125

intelligent

"elevator music" in your head, p 1; faith in the upside, p 83; self-esteem, p 93

irritated

see *angry*

J

jealous

uniquely beautiful, p 14; stuck in the muck, p 71; peer pressure, p 79; totally lovable, p 96

joyful

faith in the upside, p 83; courage to dream, p 27; totally lovable, p 96

L

lonesome

real friends, p 45; life changes, p 15; loss, p. 51; being a good friend, p 45; weaving a safety net, p 122

lost

in a crisis, p 19; real friends, p 45; feeling different and alone, p 93; problem management, p 113; finding support, p 121

lovable

totally lovable, p 96; belonging needs, p 80

loved

real friends, p 45; listening well, p 65; finding support, p 121

M

mad

see *angry*

messed up

about changes, p 15; about friends, p 45; a crisis, p 19; about sex, p 101; about parents, p 78

N

needed

real friends, p 45; listening well,

p 65; giving and getting help,
p 59; over-helping, p 63; weaving
a safety net, p 122

nervous
what is stress, p 109; about
change, p 15; about sex, p 101; in
a crisis, p 19; why worry, p 129

O

open
totally lovable, p 96; trust, p 125

optimistic
faith in the upside, p 83; courage
to dream, p 27; getting a new
coach, p 4; totally lovable, p 96;
why worry, p 129

overwhelmed
stress, p 109; with change, p 15;
by a crisis, p 19; getting support,
p 121

P

paranoid
people I can trust, p 125; getting a
new coach, p 4; stress, p 109

powerful
see *confident*

powerless
see *defeated, depressed*

pressured
peer pressure, p 79; by parents,
p 75; stress, p 109; having
feelings, p 37; real friends, p 45;
why worry, p 129

pretty
see *beautiful*

put down
totally lovable, p 96; real friends,
p 45; getting a new coach, p 4;
also see *angry*

R

rageful
see *angry*

rejected
real friends, p 45; weaving a safety
net, p 122; totally lovable, p 96;
people you can trust, p 125;
anger, p 7

relaxed
why worry, p 129; faith in the
upside, p 83

resentful
see *bitter*

respected
totally lovable, p 96; weaving a
safety net, p 122; people you can
trust, p 125

S

sad
having feelings, p 37; finding
support, p 121; also see *depressed*

safe
people you can trust, p 125;
weaving a safety net, p 122

shamed
stuck in the muck, p 71; also see
defeated

special
self-esteem, p 93;
self-acceptance, p 87

stressed-out
what is stress, p 109; why worry,
p 129; "elevator music" in your
head, p 1; problem management,
p 113

strong
see *confident*

stupid
see *dumb*

T

tense

what is stress, p 109; why worry, p 129; also see *stressed out*

threatened

see *afraid*

U

ugly

body image, p 13; being loved for breathing, p 90; getting a new coach, p 4

uncomfortable

having feelings, p 37; ways to escape feelings, p 40; anger, p 7; stress, p 109; loss, p 51; types of feelings, p 42

unimportant

totally lovable, p 96; getting a new coach, p 4; accepting yourself, p 87

unloved

feeling different and alone, p 93; finding support, p 121; people you can trust, p 125, also see *loved*

unsure

finding support, p 121; faith in the upside, p 83; also see *confused*

upset

stress, p 109; about change, p 15; about a crisis, p 19; why worry, p 129

V

valued

being loved for breathing, p 90; totally lovable, p 96; real friends, p 45; faith in the upside, p 83

vulnerable

people I can trust, p 125; weaving a safety net, p 122

W

worried

why worry, p 129; worry tapes in your head, p 1; worry and exercise, p 20; stressed out, p 109

worthwhile

see *valued*

Now you can use *Feed Your Head* to form youth support groups!

The Caring Circle Curriculum
by Earl Hipp; illustrations by L.K. Hansen

The Caring Circle is a complete curriculum that counselors, teachers, youth ministers, and other youth organizers can use to develop broad-based support groups for young people ages 12 and older. Use it with *Feed Your Head* to promote positive youth development. Included in the curriculum:

The Caring Circle: A Facilitator's Guide to Support Groups
This manual, for both beginning and experienced support group facilitators, explains the ins and outs of creating and managing support groups. Topics include the qualities and roles of a facilitator; common facilitator "traps"; the stages of support group development (forming, storming, norming, performing, and closing); how to manage the group; and how to run meetings using the book, *Feed Your Head: Some Excellent Stuff on Being Yourself* by Earl Hipp.

Thirty-Eight Great Handouts
These handout masters can be copied and distributed at group meetings as instant discussion starters. They are keyed to chapters in the book, *Feed Your Head,* and cover The Human Volcano and Other Faces of Anger, What Is a Friend, Why Some People Use Drugs, Peer Pressure, The Courage to Dream, Discovering Feelings, "Perfeckshunism," Faith in the Upside, Warning Signals and 24 other topics. The handouts can be saved by group members and bound together as a journal charting their personal growth. Also included are 6 handouts to assist the facilitator's group management.

Caring Circle Curriculum Order No. 0847

For price and order information, or a free catalog, please call our telephone representatives.

HAZELDEN®
Educational Materials

1-800-328-9000
(Toll Free. U.S., Canada, and the Virgin Islands)

1-612-257-4010
(Outside U.S. and Canada)

1-612-257-1331
(24-Hour FAX)

15251 Pleasant Valley Road
P.O. Box 176
Center City, MN 55012-0176

Hazelden Europe
P.O. Box 616
Cork, Ireland
Telephone: Int'l Access Code
+353+21+314318
FAX: Int'l Access Code
+353+21+961269